Nigerian Odyssey

Nigerian Odyssey

Ray Kodilinye

ISBN 978-0-9568214-0-9

Prepared and printed by:

York Publishing Services Ltd
64 Hallfield Road
Layerthorpe
York YO31 7ZQ
Tel: 01904 431213

Website: www.yps-publishing.co.uk

Foreword

Professor Herbert Kodilinye by
General Dr Yakubu Gowon

G C F R., Ph.D., B.A. (Hon)., J S C S C., G O C., R A M S

I am delighted that Mrs Ray Kodilinye, for the love of her late husband, Herbert, has decided to write the story of his life, his contribution to his family, country, nation and humanity. It is a befitting tribute.

I first met Professor Kodilinye whilst Head of State in the early 1970s, not long after the end of the Civil war in Nigeria. We quickly struck up a friendship that continued until his sad passing in 2003. However, my wife Victoria remembers 'Prof' fondly from her days as a student nurse in the mid 1960s, at the University College Teaching Hospital, Ibadan.

After the Nigerian Civil War ended, the Administrator of East Central State, Dr Ukpabi Asika, was looking for someone to oversee the rebuilding of the University of Nigeria at Nsukka. He found Professor Kodilinye to be the most suitable candidate and recommended his appointment as Vice-Chancellor. The task was most challenging; Professor Kodilinye would almost be starting the University from scratch, re-establishing academic and administrative standards in addition to rebuilding the University's damaged infrastructure. Professor Kodilinye accepted the challenge with great enthusiasm and soon turned around the fortune and reputation of the university. It is because of him that many of the impoverished returning students were able to complete their studies without worrying about payment; the Federal Government agreed to shoulder that responsibility.

On relinquishing the post of Vice-Chancellor in late 1975, the new Government appointed him their advisor on health matters. He put forward a proposal to establish a specialist eye hospital – an Eye Centre of Excellence, similar to the one that he had planned, supervised and built in Libya. The hope was that the hospital would be the best of its kind in sub-Saharan Africa – a centre of excellence, gaining W.H.O. recognition. With the proposal approved, 'Prof' set about establishing his pioneering vision in Kaduna.

'Prof.' personally selected doctors, nurses, technicians and other supporting staff for the Centre and sent them abroad for specialist training. Unfortunately, subsequent Governments failed to capitalize on the Centre's value and success and, in view of this lapse, the nation failed to benefit from 'Prof's' vision. Professor Kodilinye deserves recognition for this; at the very least, there should be a plaque at that institution acknowledging his foresight and contribution to the scheme.

Professor Kodilinye was a great patriot and remained a sincere lover of his country, nation and race, despite the inconveniences that he and his family suffered in the early stages of the unfortunate Nigerian crisis of the mid 1960s. I recall many conversations between 'Prof' and I, whilst we were both living in the UK, where political and other topical issues affecting the well being of Nigeria, and her people, would be passionately debated. 'Prof' and Ray always wanted Nigeria seen in a good light, rather than the negative views held by so many.

Further details of Professor Kodilinye's exploits and contributions to Nigeria, Africa and humanity, especially in the field of Eye Medicine, have been ably told by Mrs Ray Kodilinye in this book about him. His story is worth reading, and let us all acknowledge this great Nigerian and medical visionary. To me, he will always be 'a prophet with great honour.'

A Footnote on General Dr Yakubu Gowon

On leaving office as the Head of State of Nigeria Gen. Gowan obtained the degree of B.A. (Pol./Int) from Warwick University. Thereafter he was awarded Honorary Degrees from University of Nigeria, of Ibadan and Lagos and many others as well as Honorary Degrees from Oxford and Cambridge.

Many African Universities have awarded Gen. Gowan.

General Gowon rose through the Officer rank from 2nd Lieutenant to General from 1956 -1971 becoming G.O.C. and Commander-in-Chief of the Nigerian Armed Forces. In 1966 he was appointed Chief-of-Staff having been the first indigenous Adjutant-General of the Nigerian Army 1936-65.

He played a prominent role in suppressing the first military Coup d'état in Nigeria, 1966 later becoming the Head of State and Commander-in-Chief of the Armed Forces of the Federal Republic of Nigeria 1966-1975, during which time he successfully put an end to a fratricidal civil war and brought unity to Nigeria once again. During his term of office Nigeria became a political and economic force in Africa and the rest of the world.

Gen. Gowon is presently active in N.G.O.s and charitable organisations, is the President and Chairman of the Board of Trustees and also engaged with the Carter Centre for the eradication of Guinea Worm, Malaria and tuberculosis. He is also the director/chairman of numerous companies.

Acknowledgements

My Son, Gilbert: For his encouragement throughout and for the assistance and unwavering help with the typing and editing of my book.

My Daughter, Elaine: For her unfailing encouragement and help at all times with the typing and arrangement of the text and decorative positioning.

My Son-in-Law, Alan: On whom I have relied for 'on-line' information and who designed and prepared the cover for the book.

My Daughter-in-Law, Vanessa: For her interest and encouragement not fogetting Basil Campbell their friend in Barbados, who was the first person to suggest I write my memoirs many years ago.

The Grandchildren

Russell, an old Harrovian: For his admiration of his grandfather and desire to emulate him.

Henrietta: Who loved her grandpa, bringing back memories of happy days playing with him in the garden and of course playing tricks on him.

Maria: Who is grateful to her grandfather for teaching her the values of education and the importance of taking pride in myself through life.

Matthew: Who remembers Grandpa as a disciplinarian and finally as a perfectionist.

Jessica: The last grandchild. She was a baby when Grandpa passed away. What a pity for he loved her so much.

Ricky: Deep appreciation goes to you today. Your thoughtfullness has meant much more than words could ever say. As always my best wishes in the years to come. I wish you well Ricky.

THERE WILL ALWAYS BE AN ENGLAND

THANK YOU ALL

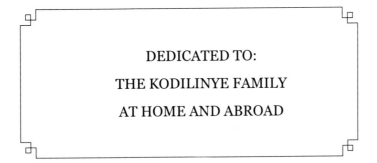

DEDICATED TO:

THE KODILINYE FAMILY

AT HOME AND ABROAD

Contents

Chapter 1

CV

PROFESSOR H.C. KODILINYE
MB CHB DO(OXON) DOMS (ENG.) FWACS FAS

Dates	Employing Authority	Position
1935-1940	Newcastle upon Tyne Eye Hospital	Resident Surgical Officer
1940-1944	Longdendale Urban District Council, Cheshire	Medical Officer of Health
1940-1944	Woods Hospital, Glossop	Honorary Medical Officer (Physician)
1940-1944	Area Casualty Services, Longendale, Cheshire	Medical Officer in Charge (Wartime Casualty
1944-1945	Central London Ophthalmic Hospital	Clinical Assistant in Ophthalmology
1944-1945	Royal London Ophthalmic Hospital (Moorfields)	Clinical Assistant in Ophthalmology
1945-1948	North London Hospital Group,Barrow-in-Furness	Honorary Consultant Ophthalmic Surgeon

Dates	Employing Authority	Position
1948-1951	Manchester Regional Hospital Board	Ophthalmic Surgeon
1951-1961	Manchester Hospital Regional Board	Consultant Ophthalmic Surgeon
1945-1961	Barrow,Furness & Westmorland Society for the Blind	Consultant Ophthalmic Surgeon
1945-1961	Iron Trades Association,Manchester	Ophthalmic Specialist Referee
1945-1961	Barrow County Borough Council	Consultant Ophthalmic Surgeon
1946-1961	Lancashire County Council	Consultant Ophthalmic Surgeon
1948-1961	Barrow-in-Furness Executive Council	Chairman Ophthalmic Services Committee
1948-1961	Ministry of Pensions & National Insurance	Consultant Ophthalmic Surgeon
1948-1958	Ministry of Labour & National Service	Consultant Ophthalmic Surgeon
1956-1961	The Army & Royal Navy	Consultant Ophthalmic Surgeon
1956-1959	The Government of Nigeria	Member Interviewing Board Nigerian Civil Service Commission in United Kingdom
1967-1969	Royal Homeopathic Hospital (Queen's Square, London)	Consultant Ophthalmic Surgeon
1967-1969	Peace Memorial Hospital, Watford	Consultant Ophthalmic Surgeon
1967-1969	Shrodells Hospital, Watford	Consultant Ophthalmic Surgeon
1967-1969	West Herts Hospital, Hertfordshire	Consultant Ophthalmic Surgeon

APPOINTMENTS HELD IN NIGERIA:-

Professor of Ophthalmology and Consultant Ophthalmic Surgeon, University of Ibadan	1961-1966
Dean Faculty of Medicine, University of Nigeria	1966-1968
At the request of the Government of Libya, Creator of the first Ophthalmic Hospital in Tripoli, Libya	1069-1970
Vice-Chancellor, Unversity of Nigeria	1970-1974
Director of Institute of Ophthalmology, Nigeria (300 bed eye hospital to serve West Africa)	1975-1985
Retired	1985

MEMBERSHIP OF PROFESSIONAL INSTITUTIONS:-

British Medical Association
Ophthalmological Society of the United Kingdom
Faculty of Ophthalmologists, United Kingdom
Oxford Ophthalmological Congress, United Kingdom
Fellow of Royal Society of Medicine
Board of Examiners in Surgery, Nigerian Medical Council

CONFERENCES:-

Attended conferences in Britain, presenting cases
Attended European Ophthalmological Congress

PUBLICATIONS:-

Published in 'Transactions of Ophthalmology'
Published in 'American Journal of Ophthalmology'
Published in 'British Journal of Ophthalmology'

HERBERT PASSES AWAY – MY TRIBUTE

PROFESSOR HERBERT CHUKUWETALU KODILINYE M.B. ChB. D.O.OXON., D.O.M.S.Eng., F.R.C.S. Ophth., F.W.A.C.S., F.S.A.N., FAS. was born in Nigeria 1909. His father was Joshua, Igwe (King), Obosi, Eastern Nigeria. His mother was a Princess. His brother was a politician. His sister was the Rev. Patience S.R.N.Eng.

Herbert passed away peacefully on 21 September 2003. I was at his bedside with Gilbert, Elaine, Alan and Vanessa.

> *"I'll walk beside you through the coming years*
> *Through laughter sorrow joy and tears*
> *And when the last call comes I'll take your hand*
> *And walk beside you to the Promised Land"*

In loving memory and admiration of my dear husband Prince Professor Herbert Chukuwetalu Kodilinye, commonly known by those close to him as Prince, I write these Memoirs at the request of many of my husband's close life-long friends, associates and colleagues who knew him from his early childhood. However it may be said that he personally would have written his memoirs more accurately, but, since he has always been a man who liked to lead his life out of the public limelight in order to perform those duties he was destined to perform, he was reluctant to do so. For me, whilst accepting this difficult *challenge*, I must endeavour at my vintage age to present the facts, events and dates as they occurred over a period of more than 70 years with accuracy if possible. I wish, therefore to apologise for any slight variations in this respect.

> *BEHOLD: how good and joyful a thing it is to dwell together*
> *in unity.*
> *Omnia vincit amor (love conquers all things)*

Herbert and I did that for 63 years of happy married life. We were 'self-contained' to use the expression of our friends. Now- I tread the path of loneliness lovingly supported by my son and daughter Gilbert and Elaine.

Time like an everlasting stream bears all its sons away
They fly forgotten as a dream dies at the opening day

MY FAMILY

My mother Rosina – 1883-1949

Born in Cornwall, daughter of a Reverend. Entered the teaching profession. Was a good pianist and above all a perfect Mother. She was an outward looking lady with a zeal for entertaining people of all races and colours and, I have to admit, for breaking the hard barrier of the burning issue in the nineteen hundreds that 'mixed marriages always fail'. For her effort I am eternally grateful. It laid the foundation for my future marriage which has proved wrong these archaic and un-Christian sentiments of yesteryears.

> *'Freedom is an indivisible word. If we want to enjoy it, and fight for it we must be prepared to extend it to every one, whether they are rich or poor, whether they agree with us or not, no matter what race or colour of their skin'*

My father Christopher – 1879-1952

Born in Newcastle-upon-Tyne in the late 1870's. He travelled extensively by bicycle (the popular means of transport in those days) from John-o-Groats in Scotland to Lands End in Cornwall, where he met his future wife (my mother). His thirst for travelling was a mission in search of historical knowledge. He was educated at Bede College, Durham from where he passed out as a fully qualified teacher. He was a member of the College tennis and cricket teams. His hobby and relaxation was drawing and gardening.

Throughout my school career he was always eager to help me with my studies, particularly in Mathematics and we burnt the midnight oil on many occasions. This was my mathematical foundation from which I gained immensely and which helped me to build my career for the future. To him I am most grateful.

Their first child Christopher Binney – 1911- 1995

Born in Newcastle-upon-Tyne. Educated at Rutherford College, Newcastle-upon-Tyne and Loughborough College, where he studied engineering. Thereafter he married and entered the teaching profession. He volunteered to join the Air Force during the Second World War and was posted to Burma, where his duty was to maintain R.A.F.war planes. He would never discuss the terrible horrors he witnessed during the war in Burma. On returning to England after the cessation of hostilities he settled in Jersey in the Channel Islands and returned to his teaching career.

Their second child, Snowie – 1913-1981

Born in Newcastle-upon-Tyne. She was an enthusiastic person, popular at school and throughout her life and enjoyed the company of others. Early in her teaching career her success as an educationalist was obvious. She was awarded a scholarship to India to observe the standard of teaching in that country and to submit a report. As a result of this she was awarded a further scholarship to visit some of the poorer areas in India, Calcutta etc. to observe the standard there. Unfortunately, however, the Second World War broke out and in September 1939 she returned to England by sea, a perilous journey as the oceans during that war were well policed by enemy submarines.

After many years as a teacher she was appointed a Headmistress in Newcastle. Shortly after taking up this post she fell ill with a crippling nervous complaint and was compelled to retire from her profession into a wheelchair, spending the latter years in a Home. She never married and passed away in 1981.

Their third child, Ray (author of the book) 1915-

Born in Newcastle-upon-Tyne. Quiet, studious type, said little-but thought more. No time for anything but studying to achieve my object-to join the teaching profession. Educated at Rutherford College, Newcastle-upon-Tyne Girls' School, having passed the entrance Examinations with

Commendation, thereby entering the College at the highest form of the first year.

Passing out from Rutherford College, I passed on to Armstrong College, Newcastle-upon-Tyne (Durham University), which became University of Newcastle in 1963. I qualified BSc in 1936 in Mathematics. I decided to make teaching my career so studied Psychology at Kenton Lodge Newcastle for 2 years after which I was awarded my teaching diploma. Thereafter it was necessary for me to do 6 months teaching experience in Northumberland – compulsory in order to be registered by Northumberland County Education Authority. I was thereafter registered.

During my time at the University I was a member of the International Club and the Student Christian Movement, attending S.C.M. conferences up and down the country. I was able through these media to meet students from different parts of the world. They were welcomed in our home by my parents, who most graciously made them enjoy *'Home from Home'*

I look back with great pleasure to those happy days as a student. Most of these friends have now sadly 'passed away' but their memory for me remains and happily there are times when I coincidentally meet with some of their relatives or friends. This gives me great pleasure.

Their fourth child, Joy 1920-

Born in Newcastle-upon-Tyne. Attended Rutherford Girls School, Newcastle, followed by Armstrong College, where she graduated BSc Science. After qualifying three years later she took up a teaching appointment in Arnold High School for Girls in Blackpool, an Independent Boarding School. She later gave up her whole time teaching career to marry.

My son, Gilbert (Prince) 1943-

Education: – (4-7yrs) Chetwynd Roman Catholic School, Barrow-in-Furness, Lancashire. (Principal – Mother Magdalene); 7 ½-11 years St

Chad's School (Lichfield Cathedral Boarding Choir School- Headmaster- Reverend Walters); Headmaster's Scholarship to Harrow School- March 1955; GCE 'O'Level in 9 subjects at the age of 14 years; Harrow School 1955 – 1960; choice of place at Oxford or Cambridge; entered Oxford University (New College) to read Classics, but changed his mind on entering to read Jurisprudence; Bachelor of Arts B.A. and Master of Arts LL.M; called to the English Bar at Inner Temple 1969. Presently Professor of Property Law at the University of the West Indies.

My daughter Elaine (Princess) 1948-

Education:- 4-8yrs Chetwynd Roman Catholic School, Barrow-in-Furness, Lancashire (Acting Head – Sister Acquinas); 8-11years Godstowe Preparatory School, High Wycombe, Buckinghamshire (Headmistress- Miss Webster); 12-17 years The Cheltenham Ladies' College, Cheltenham, Gloucestershire (Principal Miss Joan Tredgold); Reading University to read Classics B.A. Classics; London University, Birkbeck College MPhil Classics. She then qualified as a Solicitor of the Supreme Court and joined the Government Legal Service as a Senior Crown Prosecutor. She was later appointed a Senior Lawyer in the Treasury Solicitor's Department.

Chapter 2

Prince's Early Life

Prince H.C. Kodilinye, my husband, was educated at Dennis Memorial Grammar School (D.M.G.S.) in Eastern Nigeria and later in 1922 passed on to King's College, Lagos, a secondary Boarding School under the headship of Canon Peacock. There at the age of 18 he passed the matriculation examination with honours thereby qualifying to enter a British university. At that time, at the instigation of his father, he decided to study law as his future career but he later changed his mind and read medicine to prepare himself to serve his country. It should be said that during the Colonial days Nigeria, being a vast country, indeed known as 'The Giant of Africa', was suffering from a shortage of qualified doctors. This then was the incentive that finalised his determination to become a medical doctor in order to serve his country, NIGERIA. Although there were many good universities in England at that time his choice was Glasgow University in Scotland. He was amongst the first generation of Nigerians to leave home to study in a foreign land.

It is imperative that, at this point, I 'put the record straight' for sadly, there were unwarranted, ignorant and misinformed comments that Prince H.C. Kodilinye was "an Englishman who did not wish to return and help in building his country". He was a Nigerian dedicated to serve his people and as these memoirs will show, he fulfilled his ambition to the full. "Only the best was good enough for his country" was always in his thoughts. 'Nigeria par excellence' was his slogan. Professor Kodilinye's wife (the author) and children also served Nigeria in various ways as will be seen later in my memoirs.

Although he had an extremely successful and busy career as a Consultant Ophthalmic Surgeon in the United Kingdom, it did not prevent Prof Kodilinye from giving 'without charge' ophthalmic treatment to any African who sought his advice and was able to travel the long distance from Africa to consult him. Happily he was able to preserve the sight of many of these patients. In spite of pressure of work in the medical field (see Prof Kodilinye's C.V.) he was invited by the Secretary of State in the UK to become a member of the Advisory Committee on the Welfare of Colonial People living in Britain. In this capacity he was able to advise Africans who were in difficulty in various ways and helped them to obtain appointments in their home country.

One of the first Nigerians to be interviewed was a young man named P.C.Asiodu MA (Oxon) D.Litt (Hon). He entered the Nigerian Foreign Service at the age of 23 years, thereafter becoming the Chief Economic Adviser to the President of the Nigerian Conservation Foundations as well as appointments to the Chairmanship of N.E.P.A. (Nigerian Electric Power Authority) and others. As far as I am aware P.C.Asiodu is still an influential personality in Nigerian Society. He was honoured by his people with a Chieftancy title- Ijoma P.C. Asiodu. His wife, Jumoke also received a title. Chief Asiodu has written and published many books.

Our son Gilbert, a Professor of Law, followed in his father's footsteps and spent some years working in Nigeria, first in the Faculty of Laws as a Senior Lecturer at the University of Nigeria. Whilst there he wrote and published some of his best known law books, which are to this present day sought after and studied by law students in the Nigerian universities and elsewhere. He published cases in legal magazines which are quoted internationally. He later gave service to the Faculty of Law at Ahmadu Bello University for a number of years.

He is currently a Professor of Property Law at the University of the West Indies.

Renaissance 10 March 73

The Chief Justice of the Federation, Dr T.O.Elias, while attending a luncheon party being given by the University of Nigeria in his honour, said that the University ranks among the best universities in the world. The quality scope and orientation of instruction were outstanding. The Dean of the Faculty of Law, Dr C.Ogwuruke, on behalf of the University said that the academic studies had shown that the Faculty of Law had made considerable progress since its inception. The Chief Justice observed that the Faculty had associated itself with several eminent and learned Nigerians and that its staff is of international standard.

Professor Kodilinye's daughter Elaine, a Solicitor of the Supreme Court, working in the British Government Legal Service also helped in Nigeria. During her holidays in that country, which she loved, she willingly assisted with arrangements for the Convocation Ceremonies at the University each year. She was also an active supporter of the Nigerian Red Cross. Her voluntary service was much appreciated. Nigeria gained much by her unfailing service.

With my husband Professor H.C. Kodilinye I spent 26 years in Nigeria and must say that it was a wonderful experience in those days. There was much work to be done and every 'willing hand' was valuable. Hence I was able to help on a voluntary basis throughout those years and my time was well occupied.

It was in 1928 when the young man Herbert Kodilinye set sail for the United Kingdom, 'the land where the streets were paved with gold'. This was the ambition of many Nigerians at that time. He bade farewell to his family and friends (his mother had lost her life some years previously in an accident at sea). It was a tearful parting but his father made it quite clear that he would live to see his son return. Travelling alone Herbert was a passenger on a cargo ship which as would be imagined did not provide either the comfort or luxury of a passenger liner, but in the early part of the 20th Century cargo ships were the only means of travel between Nigeria and the United Kingdom, some two thousand miles away, and of course, took much longer.

He arrived in Liverpool weeks later and proceeded to travel alone by railway the 350 km to Glasgow in Scotland. Here he was met by the Bishop of Glasgow (Bishop Derbyshire) who became his mentor throughout his stay at the University. So close was their friendship that he dined with the Bishop in the Manse every Sunday.

Herbert's friends in Glasgow later in Canterbury
Lady Campbell (left) and Lady Cassidy

Hebert's quality of character soon became evident for he was chosen to be the 'Server' to the Bishop of Glasgow at all religious services in the Cathedral, later becoming a lifetime member of the Guild of Servers. The quality of his voice later enabled him to become a member of the Cathedral choir. Incidentally, he retained his singing voice throughout his life. It was his custom every Sunday to sing hymns whilst I accompanied him on the piano.

During his stay in Scotland he made, apart from his fellow students, many friends, two of whom were Lady Campbell and Lady Cassidy, who helped him in various ways to settle into his new life away from home. Reading the references which appear below it will be realised that he was a young man of high standards in all aspects of his life and held in high regard by all those with whom he had connection during his six years of study:-

FROM THE BISHOP OF GLASGOW AND GALLOWAY

> 14 Cleveden Crescent
> GLASGOW W2
> 4th April, 1935

I have much pleasure in bearing witness to the high character, industry and abilities of Dr Herbert Kodilinye.

I have been in close touch with him during his course as a student at the University, and I can say with intimate knowledge that he has studied most diligently to make himself proficient in his profession, and has shown throughout the period exemplary conduct, a cheerful disposition, and untiring industry.

(signed) JOHN RUSSELL DARBYSHIRE
Bishop of Glasgow & Galloway

MEDICAL SCHOOL REFERENCES

Western Infirmary,
Glasgow W1.
4th April, 1935.

This is to certify that Dr H.C. Kodilinye attended my class in 1934, with so much assiduity and keenness, as to be awarded a First Class Certificate.

(signed) GAVIN YOUNG, M.B., F.R.F.P.S.

Surgeon for Diseases of the Ear, Nose and Throat

Lecturer on Diseases of the Ear, Nose and Throat, University of Glasgow.

5, Park Gardens,
GLASGOW, C3
5th April, 1935

Mr Herbert Chukuwetalu Kodilinye, who has just passed the Final Examination for the MB,ChB Degree of this University, has been known to me for several years, and has been a member of my various classes. In the Winter Session of 1932-33 he was a member of my Class of Systematic Surgery, and acquitted himself very well. During the same Session he was a member of my Surgical Clinic in the Western Infirmary, where he was awarded a First Class Certificate of Merit, with percentage marks of 62.3. During the first Winter Term, October to December, 1934, he was again a member of my Surgical Clinic as an Intensive Student in Surgery, and did extremely well in the Class Examination.

I have been impressed all along with the high character and earnestness of Mr Kodilinye, who is, I know, generally very well liked and held in high regard by his fellow students, as well as by his teachers. I am sure he will have a successful professional career.

(signed) ARCHIBALD YOUNG, BSc, CM, FRFPSG, FACS (Hon)

Regius Professor of Surgery, University of Glasgow.

---

7 Grosvenor Crescent,
GLASGOW, W2
2nd April, 1935.

It gives me much pleasure to express the high opinion I entertain of Dr Kodilinye, who was a most industrious student. In many of his classes he took a prominent position in the Honours List, which testifies to his ability and industry. He possesses a sound all round knowledge of his profession, so that I have great pleasure in recommending him very heartily.

(signed) JOHN M. MUNRO KERR

Emeritus Regius Professor of Midwifery, University of Glasgow;

President, Royal Faculty of Physicians and Surgeons of Glasgow.

---

12 Somerset Place,
GLASGOW C3,
4th April, 1935.

Dr Herbert Kodilinye was a student in my classes of Practice of Medicine and Clinical Medicine. From personal knowledge I have formed a high opinion of his character and ability, and I have pleasure in recommending him for a medical appointment.

(signed) T.K.MONRO, MA, MD, FFPSG,

Regius Professor of Medicine in the University of Glasgow;

Senior Physician to the Western Infirmary, Glasgow.

Herbert qualified M.B.ChB Glasgow in 1935 having completed his course in medicine with distinction and took up his first appointment as a junior doctor (Senior Registrar) in St Mary's Eye Hospital, Newcastle-upon-Tyne. He joined the International Club, a social meeting point for University students and it was there that I made his acquaintance whilst still a student myself in Newcastle.

It was his experience in St Mary's Eye Hospital which influenced him to study Ophthalmology further. In 1940 he settled into general Practice in the Manchester area where we were married in that year. He combined his duties as a General Practitioner in a busy practice with studying Ophthalmology and qualified D.O.M.S England and D.O.Oxon within three and a half years.

The Second World War broke out in September 1939 and from then through the following years life was pretty grim. Men of age were conscripted into the Forces or volunteered to serve whilst the women took over work in the munitions and other factories. It is interesting to note that on order of the U.K Government all iron railings in and around property private or public were removed and transported to the munitions factories in order to manufacture the necessary weapons for war. Every citizen willingly sacrificed in many ways towards the success of the conflict with Germany. Added to this was the severe rationing of essential foods, some of which lasted until 1960, long after the cessation of hostilities.

The Luftwaffe raids on Britain did a great deal of damage to our cities, which had to be rebuilt after the war ended. It was on Christmas Eve in 1942 when we in the Manchester area suffered a very severe bombardment of incendiary bombs. My husband, as the Medical Officer of Health and Chief Air-raid Warden was responsible for the care of the injured during the air-raids and I as a member of the Red Cross played my part in tending the wounded. Although the raids continued in various forms throughout the war, Britain was not daunted and when in 1945 peace was declared there were great celebrations throughout the country and reconstruction following the heavy damage to our cities began.

'PEACE AT LAST' filled everyone's hearts with joy and hope for the future. Evacuated children returned home to their parents, air-raid sirens were silenced, there was no more living in and out of air-raid shelters or Underground stations by day or through the night, and of course no more wearing of gas masks- life could now return to normal. 'From hence let fierce contending nations know what dire effects from civil discord flow'

'The debt to our airmen. The gratitude of every home in our island, in our empire and indeed through out the world except in the abodes of the guilty goes out to the British airmen who, undaunted by odds, unweakened by their constant challenge and mortal danger, are turning the tide of world war by their prowess and their devotion. NEVER IN THE FIELD OF HUMAN CONFLICT WAS SO MUCH OWED BY SO MANY TO SO FEW. All our hearts go out to the fighter pilots, whose brilliant actions we see with our own eye day after day but we must never forget that all the time, night after night, month after month, our bomber squadrons travel far into Germany, find their targets in the darkness by the highest navigational skill, aim their attacks, often under the heaviest fire, often at serious loss, with deliberate, careful precision, and inflict shattering blows upon the whole of the technical and war-making structure of the Nazi power.'

(from a speech by Sir Winston Churchill, Prime Minister, 1940-1945, who led his country in the Second World War)

It was the end of the war which prompted my husband to move out of General Practice and take up an Ophthalmic appointment with a view to giving the best service possible to Nigeria, bearing in mind the extent of blinding diseases in Africa. He was appointed to the post of Consultant Ophthalmic Surgeon in the No 1 area of Manchester, which covered a very wide area from Carnforth to Whitehaven and to be the Hon Consultant Ophthalmologist at the North Lonsdale Hospital in Barrow-in-Furness, Lancashire (now Cumbria). Various other ophthalmic appointments followed between 1945 and 1961.

During our time in Barrow-in-Furness my husband treated, without charge, many Africans particularly from the West African Coast who were able to make the long journey to Britain, as well as other well known patients such as Donald Campbell, the British car and motor boat racer and owner of the famous 'Bluebird'. Campbell broke world speed records in the 1950s and 1960s and remained the only person to set about land and water speed world records up to his death in 1964, whilst attempting a further speed record on Lake Coniston in Lancashire.

Chapter 3

Our First Visit to Nigeria

As the years passed we began to cast our minds towards Nigeria and decided to take a holiday, first for Herbert to be re-united with his father, who had patiently waited for almost 20 years and secondly for me to see for myself 'life in Africa' and of course, more importantly, to be introduced to Herbert's father and family.

In March of 1948 we were ready to set sail from Liverpool together with our son, Gilbert who was 4 years of age, and complete with topi (the popular sun helmet worn by the missionaries who settled there during years of colonisation, we boarded the Elder Dempster passenger liner MV APAPA (named after the Wharf area in Lagos at that time), incidentally built and launched in Barrow-in-Furness. Many of the shipbuilders were, in fact my husband's patients so we really felt at home on board. The first port of call after 6 days at sea passing through the dreaded Bay of Biscay, where the pounding of the sea knows no limit, was Las Palmas, in the Canary Islands. We were allowed to disembark to visit the beautiful serene city, designed to accommodate passengers from the ocean liners. The sun was shining and the wharf was filled with market stalls and bustling stall-holders were ready to call for the highest price for their goods. Shopping finished it was time to re-embark by means of the ship's ladder stretching from the wharf to the deck, quite a balancing feat. 'all aboard" and the ship's horns blew loud and clear signifying our departure for the 2nd port of call, Freetown in Sierra Leone.

After six days at sea we were approaching the West African coast and, of course, the tropics. Meanwhile the ship's crew had discarded their dark winter uniform and instead appeared in brilliant white. At the same time the passengers were served with cold drinks on the deck each morning at 11.00 a.m. instead of the hot soup which we had enjoyed since leaving Liverpool. We realised that we were now in the tropics. Yes! excitement was building up for those who had not been to this part of the world and this naturally included me. I had an added excitement for this time we were to disembark along different parts of the coast where I would meet again many of my old University friends with whom I had studied and joined in sporting events. They had returned home to their native lands after completing their university courses and had become proud owners of a university degree from the United Kingdom. They were doctors, lawyers, scientists, engineers and many other disciplines.

As the water in Freetown harbour was very shallow, the Liner anchored a little distance from the shore. Passengers wishing to land had to disembark in to a small boat which ferried them across to the wharf. The first thing I noticed on landing was the beautiful sandy seashore, almost silver in colour, with the deep blue waves of the Atlantic Ocean lapping over it.

We landed safely on 'terra firma' and were met by our friends of some 20 years previous. It was a most pleasant and exciting time as we all had much to tell and enquire about and only one and a half hours in which to do it. It was not possible for me to leave without obtaining a souvenir of my first landing on West African soil, and so my search led me to a little market where I bought three boxes of brightly coloured butterflies and moths, which I have treasured throughout my life and only parted with them some five years ago. They eventually found their way to the Natural History Museum in London, where I am confident they will be preserved for many years to come.

As the sun began to set and night was falling (twilight in the tropics is very short) it was time to return to the liner Apapa by the ferry which was standing waiting for the passengers. We were soon on board but before we set sail it was the custom for the visitors leaving Freetown by the liner to throw into the water any coins for which they had no further use. Many children of all ages who had been taught from infancy to swim well were waiting at the wharf and dived into the deep water to recover as many coins as they were able to help buy much needed food. As we waved 'good bye' from the deck to our friends their shadows gradually mingled with the twinkling lights of the harbour and finally went out of sight.

Takoradi in the Gold Coast was the next port of call and only two days sailing from Sierra Leone. The nights were getting hotter and as we sailed further from land into the depths of the ocean the sea began to swell and the ship rolled from side to side, for it had been built in the 1940s before stabilisers were fitted. We all made a hasty retreat to our cabins and hopefully sleep, depending on the high waves, only to be awakened by the ship's bell at day break announcing our approach to the harbour.

Here again we disembarked to make a short visit inland. We made our way by taxi to visit our friends Chief Justice McCarthy and his wife in Accra. Interesting exchanges of views took place over lunch in their home. Justice McCarthy was a good friend of ours and when he visited England he stayed with us in our home in Barrow –in–Furness. As we said 'au revoir' to the Gold Coast my last thought was how lush and green the vegetation was in this part of the West African coast-but it was the sunglasses which I was wearing that gave the magical touch. An optical illusion!

Three days later, after thirteen days at sea from Liverpool we arrived at Apapa wharf in Lagos. It was crowded with people, men women and children dressed in traditional costume dancing and singing to the rhythm of the frenzied beat of the drums. For me it was the beginning of 25 years of African dance, a far cry from the ballroom dancing which I had been used to when Victor Sylvester played on Saturday evenings. I knew that I was going to enjoy all that Nigeria had to give.

We were met when we disembarked, by members of the extended family and taken to stay at a Guest House in Apapa (Lagos) at the invitation of Dr Nnamdi Azikiwe, who was later the first President of the Republic of Nigeria (1963-1966). Arrangements for our travel to Onitsha, the nearest town to our final destination were already completed.

The following morning we left by the scheduled plane, a small Dove aircraft, accommodating about 12 passengers. It was the month of April and the 'rainy season' had already begun. The flight was pleasant and the sun was shining until we ran into an electric storm as we approached the river Niger. It was so fierce that all on board were silenced with fear lest we should be brought crashing into the windswept depths of the water. For my husband, Gilbert and myself, it was a terrifying few moments, but God being on our side, the pilot, accustomed to such conditions, made a desperate swerve as he reduced height and in seconds we were heading back to Lagos, leaving behind the crocodiles we all imagined were waiting for us, jaws open. We thanked our Master for this lucky escape.

Eternal Father strong to save
Whose arm hath bound the restless wave
Who bidst the mighty ocean deep
And calm amidst its rage didst sleep
O hear us when we cry to Thee
For those in peril on the sea

O Christ whose voice the waters heard
And hushed their raging at the word
Who walkedst on the foaming deep
And calm amidst its rage didst keep
O hear us when we cry to Thee
For those in peril on the sea

Safely back in Lagos we had time to reflect and decided not to make this flight again but to travel east by land, some 300 hundred miles away on rough roads.

We spent the night in a little chalet just outside Lagos. The chalet was in deep wooded area, there was no electric light just kerosene burners and outside in the darkness we could hear the frightening noise of the rattle snakes. A good friend of my husband, Mr Isaac Iweka provided a Buick motor car and driver for us to make the long journey by road. To avoid traffic we set off at midnight the following day. Some two or three miles along the muddy forest road with no lighting and only the road to guide us the car struck an object, which turned out to be a wandering goat. The driver did not stop for he was used to this situation, he carried on oblivious as to what had happened.

Eventually we left the forest and were on the main road in the Mid-West travelling over rough roads and negotiating narrow broken down bridges which spanned the streams in which were the remains of several heavy vehicles which had overturned into the water. At about 3 p.m. that afternoon we reached Benin City, capital of the Mid-West. We stopped at a small hotel to refresh ourselves and have a good ablution for we were heavily peppered with red dust which had been blown in through the car windows on this long journey. We set off again to reach Asaba before darkness fell but our trials had not ended even then, for we were confronted by a large tree which had fallen and completely blocked the road. There was no alternative but to take another pathway into the forest. This we did and with a sigh of relief eventually found our way out onto the main road once again. From then on our journey proceeded smoothly until we reached Asaba, the last town on the west bank of the River Niger. Now we must cross the very river which could have claimed our lives only 3 days earlier.

With the aid of binoculars we could see a seemingly endless stretch of people waiting to greet their 'son of the soil' returning home to his native land after a sojourn of 18 years and what was more, with his family. There was frenzied dancing, beating of drums and firing of heavy guns in the distance on either side of the river, all kept in order by a strong force of police in uniform with horse-whips-not guns. A boat called the Shanahan was anchored at the wharf.

Justice Michael Ajegbo was anxiously awaiting our arrival to welcome us and escort us aboard the boat. he produced a pair of binoculars to enable Prince and his family to view the dense mass of people dancing to the beat of the drum, children as well as adults, a sight I was to experience many times during my 25 years in Nigeria. I was already used to the rhythm and often found myself trying to keep time with my feet.

Once again uniformed police were present in large numbers to control the excited crowd awaiting our disembarkation. The nearer we approached the opposite bank the greater seemed the crowd. It was an awesome sight. I was in a state of trepidation for I had never been amongst such a large group of people before. As we approached the opposite shore the canon started to fire 21 salvos as is done in England (Nigeria being a British colony at that time). We reached the shore and disembarked. many limousines were waiting in line. They were large and clumsy in the nineteen forties. A terrific roar went up from the crowd. Their son was back on Nigerian soil. He was no longer 17 but a man in his thirties. Gilbert a small boy of four years dressed in a white shirt and grey short trousers, white socks and shiny black shoes, complete with tie stepped down only to be immediately picked up and held aloft to be shown to the crowd who were ecstatic with delight. He was handed from one pair of hands to another over the heads of the crowd to make sure everyone saw him and touched his hand to say 'welcome'. I must say that Gilbert basked in the adulation. I was petrified and happy to be shepherded into the first car, but the car was unable to move until the bonnet and roof of the limousine was cleared of excited onlookers, who had clambered on the car for a better view. Meantime Justice Ajegbo handed Gilbert into the car to my great relief. Drumming and dancing continued throughout the night. Slowly the line of cars was able to move away whilst the crowd were held back by the police armed with horse-whips to keep the exuberant people in check. Now out on the road in Onitsha we sped along reaching our final destination

It was a very extensive compound in the centre of which was the Palace. The boundary was surrounded by all variety of trees and bushes in bloom. There were scarlet flame trees and golden flowered trees and the beautiful coloured spider plants. Mingled with such an array of colour were the ever popular palm wine tree which provides the celebratory drink palm wine and the Kola trees providing nuts which are broken and given to guests meaning 'welcome'. This was the custom at that time in Nigeria and as far as I am aware this welcome procedure still exists.

In the centre of the courtyard were gathered the family and the extended family and as always there were happy little children to complete the picture. They were all gaily dressed for the occasion in their brightly coloured wrappers resplendent with their gold accessories. Alongside were the most important, the horn blowers, the instruments of whom I can only describe as being for size and shape like the Swiss Yodellers from the mountains. The blowers' horns of course were made from ivory and no doubt elephant tusks a valuable commodity. The message they were blowing was I would imagine 'welcome'. Sitting on the balcony was the most important person the Igwe (King), Herbert's father. He was a tall strongly built figure dressed in his full regal gown and crown. We made our way up. Herbert was the first to be greeted. It was a wonderful embrace from a great man whose son had been in England for 20 years studying medicine and had become a Consultant Ophthalmic Surgeon and had a son and heir. I thought the welcome would never end. Tears flowed profusely 'tears of joy'. But then 'yes' the Igwe lived to see his son return home as he had promised but sadly could not see him for he had unfortunately gone blind. How ironical.....
We were deeply saddened for the Igwe's sight could have been restored had Nigeria been equipped with the so necessary ophthalmic service. Blindness is one of the commonest afflictions in Nigeria.

It was now my turn to have the Igwe's blessing and I was given the title 'Princess'. I would like to add at this point that when I married in 1940 I was not aware that the groom was a Prince. It was a short while afterwards that his secret was released and I appreciated this sentiment. The ceremony, the partaking of the Kola nuts and Palm wine was now performed. The horn blowers continued their 'welcome' music whilst the guests clapped, danced, waved their flags and generally made merry well into the night. Three days of celebration followed and we were introduced to many distinguished guests from other parts of the country. They had come to greet us as a family and join the celebrations.

Our holiday lasted for 6 weeks during which time we visited much of Eastern Nigeria until I fell victim to a menière's attack which finally rendered me permanently deaf in one ear despite all consultations and treatments in Nigeria and Great Britain. It was thought to be the result of taking the anti-malarial drug Paludrene, what was known locally as the 'Sunday Sunday medicine' for it was only taken once a week and that was very often taken on a Sunday.

During these six weeks it was my intention to visit the Mission Schools. This I was finally able to do with the aid of the Nigerian Education Authority Minister, by name Miss Plumtree. Being during the colonial days she was of course an English lady. I recollected her being a short, stocky lady around the age of 50 years. She looked very severe and disciplined as you would expect. She drew up for me a comprehensive itinerary and consequently I was able to see many mission schools both Roman Catholic and Anglican situated in many parts of the country. I remember with great pleasure having the opportunity to give a mathematics lesson to pupils in Queen's College, a mission school situated in Enugu. The girls were indeed most receptive and I formed the opinion that the education of the children in Nigeria during the colonial era was of a high standard although, if I am to compare the two religious institutions, I would say that the Roman Catholic schools were better equipped than those of the Anglican. Perhaps the reason being that they were financially in a better position.

Later when we returned to Britain I was invited by St Georges Church in Barrow-in–Furness to give the opening address at the anniversary of the SPG (Society for the Propagation of the Gospel). This gave me the opportunity to give my first-hand impression of the work of the missions in Nigeria in respect of their educational system. It was well received and went to press.

Our mission to Nigeria being completed it was time to say farewell to the Igwe and all the friends we had met during the 6 weeks holiday. Returning to Lagos the capital by car was uneventful except for a few minor incidents due to the poor state of the terrain and the broken bridges that spanned the streams. That was the norm at that time.

Within a few days of reaching Lagos we set sail in the Apapa, the second Elder Dempster Liner to be built in Barrow-in-Furness. The 13 day journey back to Liverpool gave us time to re-organise our life and that of the children for our daughter, Elaine, our second child was born only a few months later in Barrow-in-Furness. We decided that it was necessary that they should be settled into boarding schools in England before we could return to Nigeria to help build the country as was our promise and intention. Unfortunately this had to be somewhat delayed owing to the passing away of my parents within a year of each other.

MAY THEIR SOULS REST IN EVERLASTING PEACE

Chapter 4

End of Work in Britain

The task of uprooting many years of study and employment in the United Kingdom was of great magnitude and in addition to this we were to leave our son and daughter behind to complete their education without the support of their grandparents. Before our departure Her Majesty Queen Elizaboth II, who knew much about my husband, his father and his background invited us to Buckingham Palace Garden Party in recognition of his immeasurable service to the United Kingdom in the medical field.

The Government felt the end of his service was a great loss to the country and offered to retain the posts which he held should he wish to return to the U.K. at any time in the future. He had rendered various services before and during the Second World War and thereafter. (see Prof H.C. Kodilinye C.V.) To return to work in Nigeria was imperative, we had made that promise and we must honour it- together we did so. By the time we were ready to leave the United Kingdom our son entered Oxford University and daughter was ready to start her secondary education at the Cheltenham Ladies' College, a boarding school in Gloucestershire.

The Lord Chamberlain is
commanded by Her Majesty to invite

Doctor and Mrs H. C. Kodilinye

to an Afternoon Party in the Garden of Buckingham Palace
on Thursday, the 11th May, 1961, from 4 to 6 o'clock p.m.
(Weather Permitting.)

Morning Dress or Uniform or Lounge Suit.

Chapter 5

Nigerian Independence

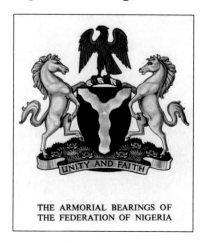

THE ARMORIAL BEARINGS OF
THE FEDERATION OF NIGERIA

THE NIGERIAN COAT OF ARMS

The Nigerian Coat of Arms features an eagle mounted on a black shield which is tri-sected by 2 silvery wavy bands.

Two white chargers support the shield and at its base is a wreath of cactus spectabilis flowers cast in the national colours of white and green.

The black shield represents the fertile soil whilst the silvery bands denote the Niger and The Benue Rivers which form the main island waterways in the country. The cactus spectabilis flower grows wild in Nigeria. The eagle stands for strength and the chargers symbolise dignity.

NIGERIAN NATIONAL ANTHEM

Nigeria we hail thee
Our own dear native land
Though tribe and tongue may differ
In brotherhood we stand
Nigerians all are proud to serve
Our sov'reign motherland

Our flag shall be a symbol
That truth and justice reign
In peace or battle honour'd
And this we count as gain
To hand on to our children
A banner without stain

O God of all creation
Grant this our one request
Help us to build a nation
Where no man is oppressed
And so with peace and plenty
Nigeria may be blessed

THE PLEDGE

I pledge to thee my country
To be faithful loyal and honest
To serve Nigeria with all my strength
To defend her unity
And uphold her honour and glory
So help me God

In October 1960 Nigeria, like the gold Coast (Ghana) before it, was granted Independence from British rule, much to the delight of the Nigerians at home and abroad. There was a stampede of those living overseas to return to their country to join in the celebrations. We were to be there too. Dr Nnamdi Azikiwe, the Governor General in Nigeria at that time and a personal friend of ours invited my husband and me as well as our two children to be present as Government guests to the celebrations on this wonderful occasion.

We sailed from Liverpool in the M V Aureol, the newest of the four passenger liners built for Elder `Dempster lines in Barrow-in –Furness shipyard, Lancashire. We stayed in Ebuta Metta, a district in Lagos the capital as Dr Azikiwe's personal guests and consequently were able to attend and enjoy all the activities which were organised for the occasion. It was heart-warming to see the real joy and anticipation of the Nigerians who had travelled from all parts of Nigeria, the north, the east and the west to take part in the celebrations in unison with ecstatic hope for the future of the country.

The activities lasted for three days, after which it was necessary for us to return to Britain to carry on with our work.

Shortly after our return to Britain, Dr Azikiwe was to visit the United Kingdom and was as usual to be a guest in our home. Professor Kodilinye thought it appropriate at the time to hold a further celebration in Barrow-in-Furness to show gratitude to the British colonisers for their effort and sacrifice to build a better Nigeria.

The Mayor of Barrow was delighted to arrange such a function and called upon the Town Clerk, Laurence Alan for assistance. The Town Hall was selected as the venue and work was immediately commenced to present Nigeria in all its forms, the people, the wild life, the architecture, the costumes, the arts and crafts depicting Nigeria's history, industry, agriculture, educational system, Nigerians at play, dancing, singing and riding at traditional ceremonies were not forgotten. It was all there on display. Most important of all, the Nigerian flag flew over the Town Hall for 3 days. It was an unusual but imposing spectacle.

Mayors and their entourages from the towns in Lancashire, together with Government, Educational and Church dignitaries and of course representatives of the major industry of the town, shipbuilding were invited to the reception given by the Mayor of Barrow-in-Furness in honour of Dr Nnamdi Azikiwe PC (Privy Councillor), the Governor-General of Nigeria. The celebrations lasted for 3 days and during this time the doors of the Town Hall remained open for members of the public and schools who wished to visit the displays.

Chapter 6

Work Starts in Nigeria

When we decided finally to leave the UK we travelled in the 'M.V.Aureol' in November 1961. Sailing out from Liverpool at low tide we passed through the Menai Straits into the English Channel and south into the Bay of Biscay, the rougher part of the journey after which the passengers had developed their 'sea legs' and were ready to enjoy all the activities which the luxury liner provided for the 13 days at sea.

As travelling by air was not a popular form of transport to Africa from the United Kingdom in the middle nineteen hundreds there were many young Africans returning home by boat after completing their studies as well as many VIPs, to mention only a few :- Sir Milton Margai, the first President of Sierra Leone, Dr Hastings Banda from Nyasaland (later Malawi) who became the President for Life in Malawi (he later created a boarding school which he called the Eton of Africa, a replica of Eton College, Windsor, UK), Sir Hugh Mackintosh Foot, Chief Secretary of Nigeria 1947 – 50, Sir Mellanby and Lady Mellanby, former Principal of UCH, Ibadan, and many more illustrious passengers. There were various types of deck games, a swimming pool, and a cinema and Dinner dances in the evening to entertain the passengers on the long journey from Liverpool to Lagos. Morning and evening religious services on Sundays were conducted by the Captain and as there was no organ I was invited to accompany the hymn singing by playing the piano. This gained me the 'status' of a missionary, but they did not know that nothing could have been further from the truth.

We arrived at Apapa Wharf in Lagos, said 'farewell' to the many friends we had made on board and proceeded by road to Ibadan, the largest town in the Western region of Nigeria, settling into Sankore Avenue, a professorial house on the University of Ibadan campus. University College Hospital (UCH) campus was a short distance away. The hospital, built around 1948, was established in conjunction with University College, London. It was an extremely imposing building, still operating at the time of writing and was at that time staffed with highly qualified British doctors along with many equally qualified African staff. Within a year my husband had created a Chair of Ophthalmology and ran the department as Consultant Ophthalmic Surgeon and Professor of Ophthalmology from 1961–1966.

As mentioned before in October 1960 Nigeria became a democratic state under the Governor-General Dr Nnamdi Azikiwe or Zik as he was commonly called. He was one of the leading figures of Nigerian Nationalists (see personalities). Sir Alhaji Abubaka Tafawa Balewa became the Prime Minister. This was the beginning of what was known as the First Republic and was the beacon of hope for Nigeria.

Sadly this was not to be for many factors militated against it and in 1966 a military coup d'état ousted Zik from power. The coup is still vivid in my memory for its final preparation 'spilled over' into a dinner party held on the University campus by one of the professors. Herbert and I together with many other guests were invited and attended not aware of what was imminent. Jovial conversation took place but it was evident that all was not well in the country. Later a group of the invitees left the party after dinner and did not return. When the function finally ended we all bade farewell to the guests and returned home in the early hours of the following morning.

At daybreak University medical staff who normally travelled daily to the University College Hospital some two or three miles away were prevented from leaving the University of Ibadan campus where they lived. Road blocks mounted and guarded by armed soldiers had been set up outside the gates to prevent any movement of the population. The news had apparently been broadcast earlier that morning that a coup had taken place the previous night. Nigeria was thrown into confusion for many of the country's leaders had been killed in the coup. This included the Prime Minister, Sir Alhaji Tafawa Balewa, Sir Ahmadu Bello Saudana of Sokoto, the Premier of the northern region, and Samuel Akintola, Premier of the Western Region, as well as several high ranking northern army officers. The governing of the country was immediately taken over by Johnson Uguiyi Ironsi from the Eastern region who became the Head of State. He proposed the abolition of the Federal system of government in favour of a unitary state.

This prompted, within a short space of time, a counter coup in which (General) Ironsi who was staying at Government House in Ibadan was killed and the Ikeja Airport at the capital was seized by the army. Several Eastern military officers were also killed during this counter coup.

Ironsi was replaced by General Yakubu Gowon the youngest Head of State at the age of 32. He became the Head of the Federal Military Government and Commander in Chief of the Armed Forces from 1966 – 1975. He was a devout Christian and consequently was widely accepted throughout the country. For a time the country remained stable.

Although life seemed to return to normal the underlying distrust between the Regions led to the movement of their populations back home. The East felt unwanted in the north where they had settled many years previously, and returned to the East, while many northerners returned to the north from other parts of the country and those from the west went back to the west. Nevertheless Nigeria remained united under the Federal system.

Our time in Ibadan was soon to be over for in 1966 my husband was asked to establish a Teaching Hospital in Enugu. Having built the Department of Ophthalmology in Ibadan and left it in the able hands of a Professor of Ophthalmology he accepted the offer to create the Teaching Hospital for the University of Nigeria in the East and became its first Dean in 1966.

The atmosphere remained calm for a while, although somewhat cautious. During our five years' residence in Ibadan there was little opportunity to travel. We did, however, manage to visit Kumasi University in Ghana, since the Vice-Chancellor, Dr Bafour, was a personal friend. It was at Kumasi that I was bitten by a tse-tse fly, the carrier of 'sleeping sickness', but it was Elaine's sharp eye that caught sight of the creature sitting on me. Fortunately, the treatment which Herbert carried out straightaway aborted the dreaded disease and all went well.

Another memory I have of this journey was the dilapidated state of the Russian-made Ilyushin plane in which we travelled. It could be described crudely as a 'complete bone-shaker', for it rattled throughout the journey. However, thanks to the skill of the Nigerian pilot, we arrived safely back in Lagos after the return journey.

The advent of computerisation in our lives in the 1950s created a crisis in the teaching of mathematics. By using calculus as in traditional mathematics, only simple equations could be solved, but by the use of computational maths (modern mathematics), almost any equation could be solved. Teachers could no longer demonstrate the usefulness of traditional mathematics, so the teaching and learning of the subject was suffering, and the knowledge of maths was generally deteriorating when it should have been improving. We are now experiencing the disadvantages of the introduction of computers into traditional mathematics at too young an age.

Because of this world-wide problem, a seminar on mathematics, especially modern mathematics, was held in Entebbe, Uganda in 1963 (1964). The seminar was well attended by mathematicians from all over the world and I was fortunate enough to be able to be present. I certainly learned a great deal on that occasion. While Herbert was absorbed in creating a Department of Ophthalmology in University College Hospital (UCH), I was busy teaching maths, both traditional and modern, on the university Campus.

As stated earlier, the Department of Ophthalmology at UCH was left in able hands and continued successfully.

University College Hospital, Ibadan, Nigeria

Medical staff, University College Hospital Nigeria
(Consultants, Professors etc)

Chapter 7

Eastern Nigeria

We left Ibadan in 1966 and Herbert took up his new appointment in the East immediately. He was successful in acquiring the General Hospital in Enugu, the capital of the Eastern Region, and immediately set about reorganising the Hospital into departments and wards, adding the necessary structural features. When this had been completed, he had the task of staffing the hospital before patients could be admitted. A number of doctors from UCH, Ibadan, who had returned to the East after the disturbances, were available and were appointed to form the core of the medical staff at the new Enugu teaching hospital.

At this point, it is necessary to go back in time. While on holiday in Nigeria in 1948, Herbert was invited to speak on the radio. He took the opportunity to offer parents from all the Regions who wished their daughters to train as State Registered Nurses (SRNs) in Britain to make applications, provided, as was the case with British applicants, that they had attained the necessary educational standard. The offer was open to females over the age of 18. Many applications were made within a short space of time, and preparations to consider them commenced. Those selected were placed either at the North Lonsdale Hospital, Barrow-in-Furness, Lancashire, or at the General Hospital, Lancaster. Within the following twelve months, at least fifteen nurses had started their training, a course which required three to four years to qualify.

All but one of the students were successful and gained their SRN qualification. A small minority decided to pursue further studies and to qualify in other specialist branches of nursing. Paediatrics, Ophthalmology and Radiography were popular choices. The training of these Nigerian nurses was an unforeseen blessing as they, together with the Nigerian-trained nurses, formed the basis of the nursing staff for the new Teaching Hospital at Enugu. (The Campus for the Faculty of Law was sited in Enugu). Suitable staff quarters were built and the Faculty of Medicine was then formally established by Decree. Herbert and I were given a house in River Close, Enugu, just outside the Eucalyptus Forest.

Peace, however, was short-lived, for the July Counter-Coup had unleashed massacres against the Easterners (Igbos) who were living in the Northern Region. Also, many Igbo military officers were murdered during the earlier uprising. This persecution precipitated the flight of the Igbos back to the East. I can still visualize the trains returning to Enugu from the North packed with fleeing families, men, women and children, some gravely wounded, some at death's door, and others in makeshift coffins: a sight too terrible to describe. There were others who had trekked on foot through the forest for more than 200 miles, carrying whatever possessions they could, exhausted but happy to have escaped and to be returning to their homeland.

In these circumstances, it was little wonder that the Military Governor of the East, Colonel Chukwuemeka, Odumegu Ojukwu began to make openly secessionist statements, arguing that if Igbo lives could not be preserved by the Nigerian State, the Easterners had the right to establish a state of their own in which their rights could be respected.

Relations between the Eastern Region and the Federal Government under General Gowon, were consequently strained. A meeting was held on neutral ground in Aburi, Ghana, to resolve the matter, but General Ojukwu continued his moves to secede from the Federation and on 1st June 1967 he delivered a speech condemning racism and imperialism and asserting 'our inalienable right to self-dermination'. Secession was formally declared and Ojukwu was appointed Head of State and General of the People's Army of the new State of Biafra, named after the Bight of Biafra. Waking early one morning, I heard a radio announcement:-

'A NATION IS BORN, CALLED BIAFRA'.

Strangely, I recognised the voice making the announcement. It was none other than Miriam, one of the nurses whom Herbert had trained in Barrow-in-Furness, England, in the mid-1950s. The announcement ended with the playing of the Biafran National Anthem, to the tune of Finlandia, a soothing, peaceful, inspirational and consoling hymn, one of the most beautiful ever written:-

Be still my soul, the Lord is on thy side.
Bear patiently the Cross of grief and pain.
Leave to thy God to Order and provide.
In every change He faithful will remain.
Be still, my soul, thy God doth undertake
To guide the future, as He has the past.

The Finlandia Hymn refers to the serene hymn '-------' section of the patriotic music Finlandia written in the 1890's by the Finnish composer Sibelius

THE PLEDGE

Land of the Rising, Sun
Land of the Rising, Sun
We love and cherish
Hail to Biafra Consecrated Nation Oh Fatherland,
This be our solemn pledge.

The national flag of Biafra flew boldly over the barracks in the Capital, Enugu.

The announcement was a great shock to Herbert and me, for we had no prior knowledge that this was to happen, not being attuned to the politics of the time. The act of breaking the unity of Nigeria, known as 'the Giant of Africa', and whose crest was embellished with the emblem UNITY AND FAITH', was frowned upon by the international community, although the sentiment which caused the situation was fully understood. Biafra was ready for war.

At this point, the British Government made ships and aircraft available for the evacuation of British citizens and their families living in Nigeria. They were given only two days to leave. Most left by ship from Port Harcourt. The staff at the University of Nigeria, who at that time were mainly expatriates other than British, left in haste, some said 'in their slippers', such was their anxiety to escape before it was too late. I decided to remain with Herbert, to give whatever Service I could, as I had been a member of the Red Cross in England. Within days, the Federal Government took action, and the Civil War began on the 6th July 1967. At the beginning Biafra had three thousand troops but by the end of the war it had thirty thousand. Nigerian troops advanced into Biafra in two columns. The first army offensive was through the north of Biafra, led by Colonel Shuwa and the local military units, led by mostly northern officers. They advanced on the town of Nsukka, the site of the main Campus of the University of Nigeria. Nsukka fell to the Federal troops on 14th.July 1967, only eight days after the commencement of the war, as the town was only a few miles distant from the boundary with the Northern Region. Biafra responded with an offensive into the Mid-Western State, from across the River Niger. Passing through Benin City, the Mid-Western capital, the Biafran troops in August entered Ondo State in the Western Region. At this point, they were only 130 miles to the east of Lagos, the Federal Capital. This valiant attempt greatly boosted the morale of the Biafrans.

Meanwhile, Biafra was undergoing a period of siege and the area was being blockaded. On 26th July 1967 the port City of Calabar was taken by Federal troops, thus leaving Biafra with little outlet to the sea, and when Port Harcourt fell on 19th May, the blockade was complete.

It should not be forgotten, however, that from the beginning of the Civil War the combating sides were unevenly matched, for Nigeria understandably was supported by the British Government with whom the Federal Government had an arms agreement, whilst Biafra was recognised only by Gabon, Haiti, Ivory Coast, Tanzania and Zambia.

As the Nigerian troops advanced further into Biafra, there was widespread hunger and starvation in the besieged Igbo areas. Many Nigerian authors have written extensively on the topic of the Civil War; consequently it is not my intention to enter into more detail. I propose therefore to continue with my narrative of events as they affected Herbert and me personally.

The initial attack from the North on the university town of Nsukka, led by Colonel Shuwa, ended in the complete destruction of the buildings and infrastructure of the University of Nigeria and the looting of everything that was available. The Federal troops now concentrated on the taking of the Biafran capital city, Enugu. Once again, the combat was desperately unequal, for Biafra was unable to import weapons and ammunition for its troops, or food for its starving population. Many children were dying from kwashiorkor, a disease caused by malnutrition. Far outnumbering the Biafrans, the Federal troops seemed to be aiming their air attacks on civilian areas, thus causing the deaths of thousands of men, women and children. We too were affected when one of the rockets smashed into our garden wall in River Close, destroying one of the steward's quarters. Fortunately, our steward was not in at the time. I was on the upper floor of the house and hastened to take shelter underneath the staircase. In doing so, I fell and struck my head on the concrete floor, sustaining a serious head injury. Herbert rushed me to the nearest hospital at Onitsha, 80 miles away, where I received emergency treatment. It was decided that further investigation and treatment was urgently required and, with the help of Solicitor Litumbe, a good friend of ours who was living in Cameroun, a direct flight from Douala to London was booked for us on Air France, leaving the following day. On arrival in London, I was admitted to hospital for further investigation and treatment.

God directs our path in life
The places we will go.

Chapter 8

Eye Hospital in Libya

Normally, treatment for head injury is likely to be prolonged, and recovery slow and mine was no exception. In the meantime, the Government of Libya had invited Herbert to give Service to that country by establishing the first eye hospital in Tripoli. Acceptance of the offer was an interim plan for Herbert, as we were to return to Nigeria after my recovery which, as expected, was slow.

In July 1968 we were ready for Herbert to take up the appointment and we travelled from London to Italy by train, then took a ship across the Mediterranean, via Sicily and Malta, to Tripoli, where we were surprised to be met by an armed vehicle. Our first thought was: 'Oh, no! Not another coup!' Alas, a coup had taken place, for King Idris, who had been on holiday out of Libya, had been deposed by a young colonel by the name of Gadaffi, who immediately took over control of the country. At the time of the coup, the new Head of State was just 28 years old. On arrival in Tripoli, we were escorted to the Hotel Mediterranean until the situation had settled down. All necessary arrangements for office building and provision of office staff and equipment were ready for Herbert to commence his plan for the creation of North Africa's first eye hospital in Tripoli. He was accompanied by armed vehicles each day to and from the office, and he returned to the hotel safely each evening. During that rather tense period, guests, including myself, were confined to the hotel, so we would be protected from trigger-happy soldiers searching for 'traitors'. The 'traitors' incidentally were never apprehended since they had established a roof-top hideout. To avoid these groups of soldiers who invaded the hotel each day, guests made our way to the lifts, which were operated up and down from floor to floor without stopping until the soldiers had completed their mission and left.

Shortly afterwards, when the country had returned to normality, Colonel Gadaffi made available to us a villa near the Gasuramite (Kings Palace) and gave Herbert a free hand to furnish it to our liking. When the furnishing was completed, we moved in. Thereafter we were very happy for the remainder of our stay in Libya, for the people were most welcoming and friendly. I still remember at least one Arabic word which I heard many times daily: MA'ALESH (pronounced 'Malish'), meaning 'Never mind' or 'No problem'. That word really summed up the generally laid-back attitude of the people: all difficulties were solved by the word MA'ALESH!

The eye hospital was completed in late 1969 and named the MOJAZAT EYE HOSPITAL. My information is that it still exists to serve the Libyan people, though the name has been changed. 'Mission accomplished', we said 'goodbye' to our many friends in Tripoli and returned to London.

Chapter 9

We Go Home

Meanwhile, the Civil War in Nigeria was still raging, and deaths from hunger and disease, particularly among the very young, continued to increase. Since Biafra was by now completely land-locked, no aid could enter and its people were surviving on whatever they were able to grow in their own compounds. Moreover, the airports had been bombed one by one and no longer existed. How, then, were we to return to Biafra? We felt we had to return somehow and we reminded ourselves of the old adage Fortis fortuna adiuvat ('Fortune Favours the Brave'). So we decided to return by a French aircraft flown by Caritas from Lisbon in Portugal to Eastern Nigeria or, I should say, to what was left of Biafra. No questions asked, and no answers given, we made ready.

My first reaction was to stock up with powdered milk, as much as I was able to carry aboard the plane, plus more, for I was operating in the capacity of a Red Cross member. I was desperate to save the lives of as many children as possible and this was a good way of helping. The more I could take, the more lives could be saved, I thought, so I continued to stock up until the day we left. I had a good friend, a Nigerian, who was able to make the necessary arrangements with the Operators of the aircraft to put the packages on board.

One early evening late in August 1969 we left London for Lisbon. It was dark when we arrived at the Lisbon airport, to find our aircraft parked at the far end of the runway. We did not proceed in the normal way to check in our luggage at the terminal. Passengers on this flight, about 20 in all, with their passports and luggage, were taken aside and attended to. We were then escorted to the aircraft on foot, and we boarded. Still no questions asked and no answers given. We mounted the gangway in single file and entered the cabin. As we had not previously been given seat numbers, it was 'free seating' and we sat where we pleased. There were seat belts, but most were broken; there were no cabin crew to give assistance; there was only the pilot, and no flight engineer in case of emergency. At last we realised the situation. Very quickly the gangway was removed and the pilot, a hardy-looking, middle-aged man in mufti, closed the plane door and sat down in the pilot's seat. The passengers were naturally somewhat apprehensive.

The plane was revved up, we took off, and the journey continued. As we approached the West African coast, the air conditioning began to fail, affecting some of the passengers. As this was a serious situation, the pilot decided to make an emergency landing at Banjul in the Gambia. We touched down in the early hours of the morning. After disembarking, we were shepherded into a wooden hut to await the repair of the aircraft. This was completed several hours later. Meanwhile we passengers were becoming anxious, for we seemed to be cut off in the wilderness with no seats to sit on and no food or water, and with only our chatter, and occasional laughter to entertain us. There was a collective sigh of relief when we heard the plane land some distance away. The pilot returned to the wooden hut where he had left us and we all walked back to the aircraft and boarded again, with the hope that we would complete the journey safely, and we did.

From Bathurst (or Banjul as it is now) to our destination 'as the crow flies' was about 1,500 miles. Everything went smoothly from then on, though by that time the passengers were weary and, of course, hungry. 'Almost there!', we thought, as we passed over Sao Tome, a small Island in the Gulf of Guinea due south of Port Harcourt, over which we had to pass to enter Biafra or, should I say 'what was left of it', as the ring around it had closed in further. Nearing Port Harcourt we heard once again the familiar sound of the Russian rockets, no doubt aimed at the aircraft. Our French pilot, a veteran of war-time flying, knew just the manoeuvre to make, and we safely escaped the blast and flew on without further incident to the makeshift airstrip where we landed. The airstrip was in complete darkness as Biafra was under a strict blackout at the time. Our luggage was off-loaded with the aid of torches, and the waiting cars drove us to our various destinations.

God moves in a mysterious was
His wonders to perform
He plants His footsteps in the sand
And rides upon the storm

Arriving back in Biafra to see the utter destruction the Civil War had created and the terrible suffering of its people was heart breaking. Despite their suffering, the people were as determined and resolute as ever, under their leader General Ojukwu, to win the war in order to be FREE. There was poverty, homelessness, hunger and disease and, perhaps worst of all, the deaths of many thousands of children from kwashiorkor. I wondered how the Containers of powdered baby milk which I had brought could even help. Nevertheless, I managed to distribute them to children most in need, and I prayed:-

Injustices are hard to bear
They make us want to fight
But God knows what we are going through
In time He'll make things right.

At this point, knowing that the British Government was sending to Nigeria weapons of war which were having such a devastating effect on the people of Biafra, I wrote to a well-respected Member of Parliament in Britain, known to me personally, informing him of the situation. I received a reply which gave Herbert and me at least some hope.

Between July 1967 and January 1970 there were 100,000 military casualties and between 1967 and 1970 the war claimed 500,000 starvation claimed at least 2 million according to records. In January 2000 Colonel Ojukwu reflected 'none of the problems that led to the war have been solved yet'.

On 5th January 1970 the Civil War ended and a Peace Agreement had then to be entered into between the Federal Government and the Biafrans. 'Quiet thought and contemplation unravels every knot.' Dr Nnamdi Azikiwe for Biafra and General Yakubu Gowon for Nigeria agreed to meet to discuss the conditions on neutral ground. London was the chosen venue and the two Leaders met at the Piccadilly Hotel. Also at the meeting were Chief AY Eke of the Mid-West Region, Herbert, and my son, Gilbert, who had qualified as a Barrister a few months previously. Unity was the objective, and as a result of that meeting Nigeria did indeed become UNITED once more.

It is fair to add that the Biafrans, although they were vanquished, made remarkable progress on the technological front since, during the blockade they were able to make bombs and rockets, and to guide them to their targets, and to maintain machinery and equipment in working order. Most remarkably of all, perhaps, they were able to produce petroleum by extracting and refining crude oil in their own back gardens!

Well done indeed, Biafra.

Sunday 26 July 2009. I pause at this moment in my writing to hear an announcement on the television in my flat in London the following announcement:-

We announce the death of Mr Harry Patch, the last surviving veteran of World War I, at the age of one hundred and eleven. Harry Patch never watched a film on the War or ever wished to talk about war, for he maintained that 'war is organized murder and nothing else! He was anti- war and anti-hero.'

Chapter 10

From the Ashes ...

Herbert and I spent 26 years in Nigeria and I must say that it was a wonderful experience in those days. There was much work to be done and every willing hand was valuable. Hence I was able to help on a voluntary basis throughout those years and my time was well occupied.

Perhaps the years when life was hardest, but rewarding was the period immediately after the Civil War. In 1971 General Yakubu Gowon, Head of the Federal Military Government and Commander-in-Chief of the Federal Republic of Nigeria appointed my husband as the post-war Vice Chancellor of the University of Nigeria. Although Herbert accepted it was with great trepidation,for he was a clinician rather than an administrator.

Sketch Profile – 6 March-1971

If you want the top elder Nigerian who speaks no Hausa, Igbo or Yoruba, but English, it is Professor Herbert C Kodilinye, the Vice- Chancellor designate of the University of Nigeria. He is the one Nigerian uncommitted by ties with the Nigerians, but by his great responsibility for them in office as an eye diseases specialist at the University College Hospital, Ibadan. His appointment as Vice-Chancellor of the University of Nigeria takes effect from 1st April 1971.

About 54, of moderate stature and light body build, the medical genius and eye surgeon would soon hold the toughest peacetime responsibility in Nigeria since the civil war. It is the tough job of erecting a new standard of character and learning for the intellectually inclined class of Nigerians, especially those from the war-affected areas and sustaining the light to shine into all nooks and corners of Nigeria: no longer a torch-light stood in a breeding ground to watch party states interests towards an isolationist doctrine.

RESPONSIBILITY

Will he be equal to the job? Oh, yes! Those who appointed him had done their researches well and found him the most qualified person, for many reasons, academics apart, before seeking his consent for the approval of his appointment. He is at present Professor of Ophthalmology at the University of Ibadan. He once had a short-lived release from responsibility from Ibadan to organize from scratch a Teaching Hospital in Enugu for the Faculty of Medicine at the University of Nigeria, Nsukka, between April 1967 and July of that year. He became its first Dean.

Between 1969 and 1970 he organized the eye diseases services in Tripoli, Libya, and also established the first eye hospital in North Africa outside Egypt. The Vice-Chancellor designate still remains, for record purposes, the only African medical consultant to serve with the British National Health Service, where he offered uninterrupted, distinguished service for over fifteen years. As far as first class records are concerned, Professor Kodilinye has a stock of them, most hidden within his personality. But where the exigencies of a struggling nation require first-rate services like his, as of necessity nationalist- inclined observers must needs unearth the unobtrusive professor's trump cards and negotiate him into the limelight. This was exactly what happened before Professor Kodilinye's qualities emerged unchallenged for the vacant Vice-Chancellor's post. This was how he got a top, tough job, for which he might never have got the nerve to apply, because of the flurry of limelight that attends it. Not every kind of light, as the Vice-Chancellor designate certainly is, likes to be displayed in public. But he must henceforth quickly integrate a popular protective device around his rare kind of light and accept that his fondly discretionary detachment, so far from a waiting appreciative wider public (not his professional patients), could deflect substantially the right light which youths might aspire to watch, to gauge their own success.

DISCIPLINE

The other day, I met the Professor in his office, bespectacled and clad in a modest grey suit: the embodiment of well integrated discipline and sobriety. And so the talking began. Professor Kodilinye was born in the North, although his parents came from the East. He was educated in the West before he went to Britain as a teenager for further studies, but "I am uncommitted to any of the parts of Nigeria, since I speak none of their languages". He explained that while he was growing up in the North and speaking Hausa and Nupe, his father, a marine superintendent, well educated in his time as a graduate of CMS Grammar School, Lagos, resigned his post in the North to settle in the East, and later became the Eze (King) of Obosi, near Onitsha. Later, the young Professor Kodilinye attended the Government School, Awka, from where he won a scholarship to King's College, Lagos. Thus, the opportunity of improving in Igbo language speaking was denied him and he was soon let loose in Lagos, in the Yoruba-speaking West. But four years of secondary education in Lagos was not enough to make him fluent in Yoruba. Jumping a form at King's College, the brilliant young man gained a singular exemption from the London Matriculation and admission to Glasgow University in Scotland to study for a degree in medicine. He completed his first degree in record time and became a house surgeon across the border in England. He then pursued postgraduate training in the University of London and University of Oxford, before becoming the first African consultant in Britain, purely on merit, some eight to nine years after obtaining his first degree in medicine.

For fifteen years, he was consultant to nine hospitals in the Manchester region in England, before he was persuaded to return to Nigeria in 1961 to help the country with his knowledge and experience. The Professor had thirty solid, prosperous years in the United Kingdom. He declared: "I should not have come home at all, as I was extremely successful in Britain as a consultant ophthalmic surgeon. Also, I had spent the greater part of my life in Britain and had been happily married to a white lady for more than twenty years. Also, my only remaining early inspirational parent, my father, died some five years after our marriage (my natural mother died while I was still an infant). Why should I have come home?" Later, when his wife's advice prevailed, Professor Kodilinye accepted a salary of less than one third of what he was earning in Britain, for employment at the University of Ibadan. He added:- "But for my wife's assistance and some private means in Britain to subsidize my income, it would not have been possible to come out here and live well in Nigeria, whatever one's good intentions and patriotism." However, says Professor Kodilinye, "Service is first, money is unimportant." He convinced me that, like few dons, he likes to be comfortable with his wife, beyond which he doesn't care about money. He declared: "While in Britain I had embraced English and I forgot completely whatever Hausa, Igbo and Yoruba languages I had learned in my early school days back home in Nigeria."

INSPIRATION

He told me that, apart from the early sole inspiration of his enlightened father, he appreciated the help of a great friend and 'mentor', the Bishop of Glasgow, the Rt. Rev. J.R.Darbyshire, who was very helpful to him during his time at Glasgow University, where he represented his year in the Student

Representative Council. The first son and remaining child of his father had no time for sports and games at the University as a medical student, but although he had little time for recreation, he did earn himself a name as a powerful all-round debater. Thus, he was more interested in the more subtle intellectual and mental activities than in physical sports. An enviable father of a brilliant young practicing 25-year old lawyer, Algernon Gilbert now at the British Bar and the father of a post –graduate lady student, Victoria Elaine, Professor Kodilinye sees his impending responsibility at Nsukka as just a new assignment outside his field of dedication:-medicine. Better put by him: "Service, tough responsibility, nothing else…, not money." Just what would money mean, salary wise, to one of the highest paid consultants in London until recently, when he opted for his country's home service?

THE RENAISSANCE MAY 28 1972

NEW HORIZONS AT UNN

The former Eastern Region established the University of Nigeria in 1960 and, by the outbreak of the civil war in July 1967, it had an enrolment of 2,500 students. It became 'The University of Biafra' when the region seceded to become 'Biafra'. On the defeat of the latter and the division of the area into states, it reverted to its original name, 'The University of Nigeria.' The main campus is at Nsukka and the smaller one at Enugu. Both are situated in the Igbo-inhabited East Central State of which Enugu is the capital, and the majority of students and staff are Igbo.

The university re-opened within three months of the end of the civil war (1970) under the Vice-Chancellor, Professor H.C. Kodilinye. At first, students sat on the floor or on blocks of cement. Gradually, desks, water and electric light were secured and the restoration of buildings was started. When General Yakubu, the Head of State, visited the University, he was warmly welcomed by staff and students alike. It is remarkable that the University has been able to operate under such adverse physical conditions.

The University of Nigeria had an unfortunate history prior to the civil war in 1967, for it was in the hands of the Michigan State University. The Governor-General was the Chancellor and dominated the University. The American land grant universities, with which he was familiar, were taken as a model. A constitution had been adopted which vested formidable powers in the Chancellor, in contrast to the normal practice in Commonwealth universities.

The initial opening ceremony for the establishment of the University of Nigeria was set for October 1960, to coincide with the granting of Independence to Nigeria. Buildings were hastily constructed and teaching staff recruited at the last moment, in order to meet the deadlines. A team from Michigan State University was made responsible for much of the organization and administration, together with the teaching. MSU is a typical 'land grant university' with the defects which have earned such institutions the sobriquet 'Cow College' in American academic circles.

The team sent to the University of Nigeria was recruited with some difficulty and was remarkable for the mediocrity of most members, and for their inability to grasp that they were not setting up a 'southern negro institution' in the United States. Relations between the MSU group and other colleagues were continually strained. Most severe of all their critics were the Peace Corps volunteers, idealistic young graduates assigned to the University because of their academic promise. The chaotic beginning of the University, together with its MSU management, made it difficult to recruit competent Nigerian academics. Particularly unfortunate was the continual propaganda by the MSU group concerning the 'unique philosophy' of the University based on 'service to the common man'. It was a mechanical 'parroting' of the land grant university 'sales pitch', designed to lever funds out of American state legislators.

With exceptions, land grant universities can seldom claim that they are 'any great shakes' as academic institutions, but when they approach their state legislators they make their defects their virtues. Much effort is spent in propaganda to impress upon legislators that the particular university differs from 'ivory tower' institutions in its 'service to the common man', and courses for policemen and housewives are quoted as proof of this. The average state legislator is sturdily anti-intellectual. He accepts the assertion at face value and supports the required budget allocation. The same 'sales pitch' propaganda, however, was folly in the very different circumstances of Nigeria, and confirmed the view of members of the public that the University was academically sub-standard.

The fourth quarter of 1966 brought a dramatic change in the standing of the University. The civil war was looming. Easterners (Igbos) came pouring back to their home region and non-Easterners left for other parts of the Federation. Among the returnees were many able academics, including some who earlier had declined appointments at the University under the MSU regime. At last the other Nigerian universities began to accord respect. Since the return of peace, there had been an increasingly intense debate about the future of the University of Nigeria. MSU was not asked to return. On that there was unanimous agreement.

Chapter 11

All Hands on Deck

When Herbert was invited by General Yakubu Gowon, Head of State, to become the Vice-Chancellor of the University of Nigeria, he assumed office in April 1971. It seemed a gigantic task to rebuild an utterly devastated campus. On Government orders, he was not to allow the despised MSU staff to return. Consequently, throughout his five years in office he had to cope with the sabotage and intrigue of a small group of Nigerian staff who, for whatever reason, bore allegiance to the MSU. This became more than clear to the University authorities when it was realized that periodically the campus would become flooded with foreign currency. The University Security Department was more than competent to deal with the matter and arrested those responsible, to be dealt with by the police.

Perhaps I should mention a more subtle action. The 'trouble makers' thought that I, being the wife of the Vice-Chancellor, was a source of information. One of the gardeners at the Vice-Chancellor's Lodge received a letter from a former professor who had been on the staff at UNN before the civil war, offering to send him bean seeds to plant in the grounds of the V-C's Lodge and enclosing a cheque. The gardener, not having a bank account, showed me the letter and wanted to know what to do with the cheque. The letter writer also promised to send the gardener information as to where and how he could collect parcels on a monthly basis. The plan was obvious. There was no alternative but to inform the Head Security Officer, and I did so. The Officer took immediate action.

This and many more dangerous incidents occurred for Herbert to contend with whilst rebuilding the University after the ravages of war. Herbert was a man of stalwart character and extensive knowledge and, above all, he was dedicated to the job he had in hand, as will be seen from the references given to him many years before, during his six years as a medical student at Glasgow University.

During his term of office as Vice-Chancellor he had the complete and unwavering backing of the Federal Military Government and the University Council, and he completed the job 'without fear or favour' up until his retirement.

Herbert was an innovator, a reformer and, above all, 'a WINNER.' During his five years in office as the Vice-Chancellor, the University was rebuilt,staffed, and the degrees awarded were recognized by the University of London. **WHAT AN ACHIEVEMENT!**

The university was devastated, I should say 'raised to the ground' by the Civil War in Nigeria and consequently much reconstruction work was required. The extent of the destruction was evident for when the students, whose education had been so cruelly broken, returned to complete their studies, found themselves sitting on stones for seats in an imaginary Lecture Hall. Staff were there too. Such was the devastation throughout the campus.

Funds to rebuild the University were, naturally, limited so it was the duty of all members of staff and their spouses to put 'hands to the wheel' and help in the gigantic task. Being the wife of the Head of the Institution I felt it my bounden duty to 'take up the cudgel' and I did so forthwith.

As I have already said, the civil war had left the campus in complete devastation. Buildings were ransacked, houses stripped of all fittings, bathrooms cupboards, electrical equipment, windows, doors etc.were removed. No seating remained in the lecture halls, water and electricity had to be re-installed and worst of all, the derelict campus was invaded by 'jumping snakes'. The Administrator of the East Central State, His Excellency Ukpabi Asika advised that I should not enter into such a **Spartan** life. However, I disregarded his advice and accompanied Herbert. We stayed in a hotel in Enugu until the Vice-Chancellor's Lodge was hastily made ready for us to move into.

Housing was the greatest priority after water and electricity had been installed on the campus. As soon as it was possible to open the University, the staff were accommodated in whatever housing was available whilst new houses were being built by an Italian firm, Micheletti, together with local builders. It was amazing how quickly the houses 'shot up' and the staff both former and new, many of them expatriate, moved in. The lecture halls were refurbished after the buildings were repaired and University life began in earnest. Everyone was anxious to make up for the loss of the 3 years civil war. The University was granted its Charter and its degrees were accepted by the University of London.

My duty as the wife of the Vice-Chancellor was primarily social but as time passed it was evident that much more would be expected of me. The C.E.C. (Continuating Education Centre) so called because its function was to provide extra-mural studies also had 10 guest suites to accommodate V.I.P. visitors to the University. The town of Nsukka, where the main University campus was situated together with the Vice Chancellor's Lodge, the Chancellor's Lodge and the Chairman's Lodge was some 30 miles from the Capital, Enugu. The secondary campus at Enugu housed the Medical Faculty and the Faculty of Law.

The lecture rooms were refurbished first by the University, whose funds at the time were not sufficient to cover all the needs to cope with the volume of staff and students. This being so I felt it my duty to do whatever I was able in order to resuscitate the social activities of the University since the staff and students were badly in need of putting behind them the tragedies of war including the financial devastation after the change of the Nigerian currency.

I sought and was granted, the permission of the Vice-Chancellor and his Board of Management to do whatever I could and to use the wives of staff to help me if possible.

At that time Herbert had recruited many Dutch staff to the new Engineering Faculty that he had created, and it was the wives of these staff that came to my aid willingly and we set to work. We visited various businesses, furniture factories, fabric factories etc. in Nigeria. The Dutch ladies and I borrowed vehicles and drivers from the Works Department at the University and toured many states in the country to carry this out. It was most rewarding and the more so since the goods were a donation to the University, bearing in mind the ravages of the war. Having equipped ourselves with machines, material, furniture and the like we set to work in all earnest. Within weeks the guest rooms at the C.E.C. were fitted with curtains, beds cupboards and other items.

This gave us further impetus and we moved from strength to strength. On the ground floor we arranged a dining room and kitchen where the guests could enjoy meals of their choice.

Following the completion of the V.I.P.guest rooms, we moved to the Vice-Chancellor's office and that of his secretary. At their windows we hung some elaborate gold-embroidered curtains-a gift from a Japanese factory situated in Northern Nigeria. In the C.E.C. was a very large hall which I named 'the Niger Room'. It was my aim to prepare the hall to accommodate all important ceremonies e.g. the University Convocation Ceremony Annual Dinner each December as well as other important University occasions. Many V.I.P.guests from home and abroad attended the functions.

Foreign dignitaries being awarded Honorary Degrees of the University and their entourages as well as the Nigerian Head of State and the Governors of the 12 States being awarded Honorary Degrees also attended the Convocation Dinner. This to me was a most important room for I wished to reflect the Unity of Nigeria, particularly after the signing of the re-union of Nigeria and Biafra in 1970. I commissioned a local artist to paint the emblems of the 12 States. He was able to complete 11 from copies supplied to him by the States. The last one presented some difficulty but I was determined to complete them all. I remembered that the bus service from the twelfth state, Rivers State, passed by the University on its way to the North, some 3or 4 hundred miles journey.

The young artist and I made our way out of the campus and waited on the main road for the arrival of the next bus standing under a large tree for shelter from the torrid heat of the tropical sun. After what seemed like an eternity the bus eventually appeared, lumbering and rolling along the rough road. We waved it down and asked the driver to alight to speak to us, which he was happy to do. We told him of our mission and he gladly obliged by waiting with his busload of passengers until the artist quickly drew a picture of the Rivers State emblem printed on the front of the bus and coloured it in hastily. How happy we were, for now we would be able to hang all twelve crests in the Niger Room. We gave a 'dash' to the driver for his kindness and wished him the customary 'Safe Journey'. He went on his way whistling a happy tune! We returned to the campus having achieved what we had set out to do. All twelve Armorial Bearings could now be erected in the Banquet Hall and we thanked God for our success.

Now thank we all our God
With heart and hands and voices
Who wondrous things hath done
In whom this world rejoices

The curtains were made by the female members of the Red Cross. They were green (the national colour) and trimmed with gold braid. The High Table was erected on a platform made by the works department and accommodated the Vice-Chancellor, Members of the Council, the Senate, all State Governors and those receiving honorary degrees. During Herbert's term in office Honorary Degrees were awarded to:- Genral Gowon, Sir Louis Mbanefo, Ukpabi Asika, His Excellency Nimiery, Dr Elias, Chief Justice at the Hague and others.

The Niger Room was always crowded to capacity so it was necessary therefore to provide as many tables as possible to accommodate the invitees. Elaine was usually in Nigeria on holiday each December for she had completed her studies at London University and was able with her artistic ability, to put the finishing touches to the decoration and laying of the tables for the Annual Convocation Dinner which was always, a grand affair. We thank her for the hours she spent each time preparing and executing this difficult task.

I must not forget the Police Band which accompanied all important functions on campus. They played superbly always commencing with the University Song 'The Old One-Hundredth':-

> *All people that on earth do dwell*
> *Sing to the Lord with cheerful voice*
> *Him serve with faith His praise forth tell*
> *Come ye before him and rejoice*

By now buildings were springing up all over the two campuses, student halls, staff quarters, lecture rooms, Faculty buildings, the Auditorium, the Senate House and most important, The Church, where we could thank God for His abundant Blessing.

THE RECORD 16TH NOVEMBER 1972

POGGI TO DEDICATE CATHOLIC CHAPEL

On Sunday 19th November 1972, His Excellency the Most Rev Dr Amelio Poggi, Apostolic Delegate to West and Central Africa, will perform the dedication of St Peter's Chapel to St Peter, Prince of the Apostles. Rev Dr Amelio Poggi will be assisted by Bishops from various parts of Nigeria, including Bishop Arinze, the Bishop of Onitsha, Bishop Okoye (Enugu), Bishop Nwedo (Umuahia), Bishop Usangha (Calabar), the Auxiliary Bishop of Ikot Ekpene, Bishop Obot. Two Protestant prelates-Bishop Uzodike of Onitsha and Bishop Otubelu of Enugu- will also be present.

Acting Chaplain Msgr Ezeanya said the ceremony would begin with a solemn procession leading into the Chapel. The staff, he said, is expected to be in academic gowns during the procession In the first part of the ceremony, Rev Amelio and his assistants will bless the Chapel both inside and outside. On the Chapel itself, Msgr Ezeanya said St Peter's Chapel went into construction immediately after the foundation stones were laid in 1962, and cost 50,000 pounds sterling. It was completed in 1963, a year after it had begun. St Peter's Chapel was designed by an Irish architect, O'Sullivan, and built by Italian contractors, Micheletti.

The Most Reverend Dr Aelio Poggi was a priest for 30 years before his consecration as bishop on June 16 1967. Before coming to Nigeria as Apostolic Delegate in 1970 Dr Amelio Poggi had served as Apostolic Nuncio to Rwanda and later as Apostolic Inter-Nuncio to Uganda. He succeeded Archbishop Luigio Belotti as the delegate to Central West Africa, taking up charge of the church in Ghana and Nigeria. Archbishop Poggi will be remembered by his flock for many reasons but it is for his efforts in Africanising the Catholic Church that the memories will be sweeter. In the years he has served this country eight Nigerians have been made bishops.

Vice-Chancellor U.N.N. 1971 – 1975
(Prof. H.C. Kodilinye)
Herbert

Dedication of St Peter's Catholic Chapel U.N.N. by His Excellency the most Rev Dr Amelio Poggi Apostolic Delegate to Nigeria

Group of University Graduands 1973

Chapter 12

Metamorphosis

On the 30 May 1971, Herbert gave an address in the Auditorium to the student body from both campuses (Enugu and Nsukka) to introduce himself to the students, to give them words of wisdom and comfort and hope for the future, He received a tumultuous reception throughout his address which lasted over one and a half hours. One of the features of the addresss was Herbert's outline of his plan to introduce into the Universityof Nigeria the Oxbridge Tutorial system, a well tried and accepted method of teaching in British Universities. This plan was well received by those students present, and a roar of approval reverberated throughout the hall.

On June 15, an address of welcome was presented by the University Alumni Association to Professor and Mrs Kodilinye on the occasion of a reception arranged in their honour by the Association. Many letters from members and students followed this address, an extract of which is set out together with a student's letter below.

Extracts from an Address of Welcome presented by the University of Nigeria Alumni Association to Professor H.C. Kodilinye, Vice-Chancellor University of Nigeria and Mrs Kodilinye on the occasion of a Reception arranged in their honour by the Association.

65

JUNE 15 1971

The Pro-Chancellor, the Vice-Chancellor, Deans of Faculties, Senior University Administrators, Alumni and Alumnae of the University of Nigeria, Ladies and Gentlemen: We, the members of the Nsukka Branch of the University of Nigeria Alumni Association welcome Professor H.C. Kodilinye and Mrs Kodilinye to our alma mater, the University of Nigeria, Nsukka. Mr Vice-Chancellor, Sir, We are genuinely proud and happy about your appointment as Vice-Chancellor of the University.

The task of resuscitating the University of Nigeria and reclaiming its pre-war status is formidable and Herculean. It requires an eminent scholar of international repute, an able, dynamic and humane administrator such as you are, to meet the challenge. To have, therefore secured your services now at the University's greatest hour of need should give immense happiness to all who wish our alma mater well.

Your appointment as the first substantive post-war Vice – Chancellor of the University is a re-assurance to us all, of the good faith of the Federal Military Government and that of the governments of the East Central Sate and the South Eastern State. It has also restored the much needed internal confidence and equilibrium to the University, encouraged staff to work with loyalty and thus minimized the sad phenomenon of "academic birds of passage". We are now confident that effective decisions on policy can be taken and implemented. We are therefore collectively grateful to you for accepting to serve and lead our alma mater...

OUR PLEDGE

We pledge our loyalty to you and the government of the University, and shall be ready at all times to co-operate and contribute suggestions and material aid towards the upkeep of our Alma Mater. We re-iterate our commitment to the cause of our alma Mater at all times, in view of which we re-hearse and re-enact the oath we took on our Graduation nights here at Nsukka. "To you, the University of Nigeria, our alma mater We hereby pledge our minds and hearts, in loyalty and faith to seek truth, to teach truth, and to preserve truth.

*We solemnly dedicate ourselves to that proud and noble purpose which the University has made its own – **"To restore the dignity of man"***

Once more we welcome you and Mrs Kodilinye to the University.

Signed-President

L.O.O.

Signed by Secretary J.N.A.

A letter to the Vice-Chancellor written by a second year student in the Department of Religion, President of Religious Students Association and Treasurer of the Undergraduate Union:-

J.C.M.
Bello Hall
University of Nigeria
7 June 1971

My Dear Professor

I have the gracious pleasure of welcoming you into the Campus as our Honourable Vice-Chancellor. I am very much impressed by the dignified way in which you have started to clear the 'Aegean Stable'. Coupled with this I was very much moved by your address to the whole student body on Sunday 30 May 1971. I was moved not so much by the sincere motive behind the address as by the entire behaviour of the students during the address and the later reaction and comment of the students. I was really moved to tears when I recollected that what really is moving students to misbehave is that they have never seen a sincere leader to direct them. And now they have seen a man of their heart. Please I wish God will continue to guide you in order to carry out your good projects.

By your presence I could compare with the Moses of old, whom when God wanted to make use of him was caused to be trained in the house of Pharaoh and by coming in close contact with the civilized nation of Egypt he was able to rise above the petty politicising of the Israelites and he was then able to lead his people to the Promised Land. I congratulate you that during your stay in England, you mingled yourself with the people with noble character and coupled with the noble blood you inherited as one from the royal family of Obosi, you are now able to direct the affairs of the University. Every student here is proud of you and your activities and more especially you have no political leanings or the avarice to accumulate wealth by any means, which is destroying our nation today. Judgment has been thrown to brutish beasts and man has become a wolf to man. Why? Because 'I want to become rich overnight'. With the result that most of the students here have in mind that they are here to gather the force to cheat or subdue others and get to the top. "Retaliation" is the watchword. I believe that by the good work you have started, God helping you, this nation is to be corrected through the present youth in this University. I wouldn't say much here until I stay face to face with you

[He continues with a request to meet the Vice-Chancellor in person and ends by saying]

Extend my best wishes to your wife. May the Almighty God continue to guard and guide you in all your honest endeavour.

AN ADDRESS BY THE VICE CHANCELLOR PROFESSOR H.C. KODILINYE GIVEN AT THE UNIVERSITY OF NIGERIA, NSUKKA ON CONVOCATION/FOUNDATION, DAY, 11TH DECEMBER, 1971

Mr. Chancellor, Pro–Chancellor, Your Excellencies, My Lords, Honourable Commissioners, Distinguished Guests, Members of Congregation, Ladies and Gentlemen:

This is our first Convocation since the sad event that shook the very foundation of our country. I, therefore deem it a singular honour to have the privilege as the Vice-Chancellor of the University to welcome you all to our celebrations. We are proud to have in our midst some of our most distinguished citizens especially those we are today honouring for their great distinction in public life and for their unique contribution towards the progress and welfare of this country.

It was shortly after the restoration of peace that the University was allowed to reopen in order to resume its academic function after two and a half years of total inactivity. For this opportunity to reactivate and rehabilitate the Institution, even though under the most trying circumstances, we are deeply indebted to our beloved Head of State, His Excellency General Yakubu Gowon, to our courageous Administrator of the East Central State, His Excellency Mr. Ukpabi Asika, and to our gallant Governor of the South East State, His Excellency Brigadier U. J. Esuene.

You will no doubt observe from your invitations that, apart from the Convocation which is specifically for the reception of graduates and the conferment of Honorary Degrees, we are celebrating the 10th Anniversary of our Foundation. This Celebration should have taken place last year but for circumstances beyond our control. For it was on the 7th October 1960, as the climax to the Nigerian Independence Celebrations in the then Eastern region, that Her Royal Highness, the Princess, Alexandra of Kent representing Her Gracious Majesty Queen Elizabeth II at the Independence Celebrations, formally opened this University and laid the foundation of one of the University's early buildings.

I think it is appropriate to recall briefly how the University came into existence. As most of you know, the conception of the University was the dream of our most illustrious compatriot, the Right Honourable Dr. Nnamdi Azikiwe, Member of Her Majesty's Privy Council, our first Chancellor and the first President of the Federal Republic of Nigeria. It was to him more than to anyone else that we owe our existence as a higher institution of learning. For without his great vision, without his boundless faith in his race and the future of his people, without his indomitable Spirit, without his matchless courage when the odds were against him, there would not have been this institution. On behalf of the University, I extend to him our deepest gratitude. We have no doubt that his name will be enshrined in the annals of the educational efforts of our country.

One of the earliest steps taken in the establishment of the University was the introduction into the Eastern Nigeria House of Assembly in 1955, of a bill to create a new University in the Eastern Region, a bill which was soon enacted into Law.

In 1958 a three-man team of British-American experts comprising Mr. James Cook from the United Kingdom and Dr. John Hannah and Dr. Glen Taggart from the United States arrived in Nigeria to study the feasibility of the proposed University and make recommendations. They produced a report which was embodied in a White Paper issued by the Eastern Nigeria Government on 30th November 1958. The report recommended, inter alia, the development of the University with emphasis on vocational orientation. In 1960 a contract was signed with the United States which designated Michigan State University as the American contractor to render technical advice and assistance to the University of Nigeria. The contract was to run for 10 years and has now expired. In the same year Dr. Roy Stearns came to Nsukka as the first Acting Principal but left four months later owing to illness. He was succeeded by Dr. George Johnson during whose Principalship the University was formally opened and the Right Honourable Dr. Nnamdi Azikiwe became the Chancellor of the University. On the 17th October 1960, classes began with an enrolment of 220 students and 24 members of the academic and administrative staff.

In the following year the former Nigerian College of Arts, Science and Technology, Enugu, was incorporated into the University, its buildings forming the Enugu Campus of the University. Between 1960 and 1964 there was a very rapid development of the University as the following statistical data show:

1960	1964
1 Campus	2 Campuses
220 foundation students	1,628 students
24 staff members 1,800 intermediate staff members	246 Senior Staff Members 1 junior
8 departments with 8 degree programmes	4 faculties 15 degree programmes 34 colleges and departments 1 Economic Development Institute
2 Academic buildings	35 Academic buildings
8 student hostels	18 students hostels
34 Staff bungalows	329 staff bungalows
No library	2 Libraries

It was this speed with which the University developed and the four-year degree course based on lower entry requirements that evoked sharp criticism of the University from some sections of the academic world. During this period the University embarked on a hurried and extensive building programme, constructing several new student hostels and a series of small buildings widely separated and revealing little or no functional relationship to each other or to the programme. A simple but crowded staff housing development also sprang up. In short, an initially attractive site was needlessly transformed into an architectural nightmare. The slow, deliberate pace of University development associated with Ibadan was deliberately abandoned, and the catchword became that this University like Nigeria, was 'in a hurry'.

Dr. Johnson who had been redesignated Vice-Chancellor held office until 1964 when he was succeeded by Dr. Taggart whose administration lasted until 1966. It was during Dr. Taggart's first academic year of office that the University took a major and commendable step to allay fears about its academic standards by authorizing the appointment of external examiners, a practice which is in accord with the British tradition. It was the judgment of these external examiners that alone dispelled any remaining doubts about the academic quality of the University. In 1966 Dr. Taggart left the University and Professor Eni Njoku was appointed the third Vice-Chancellor of the University of Nigeria. About a year later the University was closed as a result of the national crisis.

The University remained inactive until April 1970 when it was reopened in a state of utter desolation and ruin. The staff and students who arrived at the Campus at the time were faced with a frightening magnitude of physical and academic problems. For about six months they grappled with these problems with great courage under the direction of the Planning and Management Committee headed by Nr. Vincent Ike until Professor Ezeilo took over the administration of the University as Acting Vice-Chancellor. He also was confronted with some intractable problems of finance, of physical construction and above all of human relations. By this time a new Council for the University had been created under the Chairmanship of Mr. N. U. Akpan. These were all participants in the great task not only of physical reconstruction of the University but of rehabilitation of staff and students. They all did a yeomen job so that when I arrived at the scene in April 1971, I was heartened to see what had been achieved and encouraged in the knowledge that the same enthusiastic spirit, would accompany my administration.

To the Planning and Management Committee and its Chairman, Mr. Ike, to my valiant colleague, the Professor of Mathematics,

Professor Ezeilo, to the Council and our distinguished Chairman Mr. Akpan, to my conscientious, diligent and loyal staff both academic and administrative, especially the members of the Works Department who shoulder cheerfully the heavy task of reconstruction, to the students of the University of Nigeria of whom, I am proud to be their Vice-Chancellor and who have exhibited very high sense of maturity, discipline and civility I would like to express my thanks for their contribution in the reactivation and progressive reconstruction of this University. To our noble Chancellor, Alhaji Ado Bayero, His Highness the Emir of Kano, who, by words and deeds, has shown great concern and affection to the University, I am most grateful.

On my assumption of office most of the problems I have already mentioned were still present. At first it seemed that the challenge of the situation was greater than the prospects of matching the challenge, the complexity of the task appearing most formidable. But with great perseverance in our effort and with single-minded devotion to our task we are beginning to solve some of the problems. We have effected a good deal of the necessary repairs to the main buildings such as the Continuing Education Centre, the Administrative building, Faculty buildings and class rooms, the student hostels, most of the staff houses and most of the laboratories especially the science laboratories which are in the process of being re-equipped, thanks to the generous assistance of some of our friends overseas. Our library is gradually being restocked with the aid of Foundations and friendly governments whom I shall mention in more detail later in this address.

Although our resources both financially and academically, are extremely limited and this is widely known, we have, nevertheless, been overwhelmed by requests from all over the country for admission to the University this session. There were 11,228 applicants, 10,064 of whom were deemed to have possessed our minimum requirements, and of these only about 1,245 were admitted. The large number of applications received is surely indicative of the high esteem with which our Institution is held. We are very sorry indeed that we could not increase our admissions and would like to point out that we are in the period of reconstruction and cannot expand until the reconstruction is completed. Our total enrolment for the session is 3,356 of whom 628 are women, a remarkable increase of our women students over last year's figure which stood at 378. It is particularly gratifying to me that our girls are increasingly being offered the opportunity to acquire higher education. It augurs well for the future.

The number of post-graduate students stands at nine only but this is bound to grow as our facilities become more adequate for postgraduate training and research.

In 1963 the University awarded its degrees for the first time to 150 students of whom 139 were males and 11 females. Since then 2,645 men and women, including the 610 who are receiving their degrees today, have become graduates of the University. Of these the proportion of female graduates is 7%. During the same period, that is, 1963-71, the University has honoured distinguished men in various walks of life and there are altogether 25 Honorary Graduates.

Between 1964 and 1971, 255 diplomas have been awarded.

I would like to take this opportunity to welcome our new colleagues from Nigeria, Canada, United Kingdom and Europe. We hope their Services to this University will be fruitful and that they will make commendable contributions in their respective fields towards the development of the institution.

Last Session saw the departure of some members of our senior staff to take up appointment elsewhere. Dr. J. C. Ene took up the post of Professor of Zoology in our sister University of the Mid-West. Dr. P. o. Ogbuehi joined the same University as Associate Professor of Physics. Mr. Vincent lke was appointed Registrar to the West African Examination Council. To them we offer our hearty congratulations and send them our very best wishes for the future.

RECONSTRUCTION AND ACADEMIC ORGANISATION

It has become my lot as the first Vice-Chancellor of the post-war University of Nigeria, in co-operation with my colleagues, to review the approach of the founding fathers and Chart a course for the reactivated institution. We are mindful of the difficulties ahead but are equally resolute that we shall create out of the ruins, an institution that will be the pride of our country and a legacy worth bequeathing to succeeding, generations. An institution where our sons and daughters, will be educated in the truest sense of the word and be fully prepared to render competent service to their people and to the nation.

SITE OF THE UNIVERSITY

As I mentioned earlier there are two campuses of the University. One at Nsukka and the other at Enugu.

A third Campus at Ogoja is under active consideration. Since it is neither administratively economical nor educationally advantageous to run three campuses, we shall advise that all the faculties be concentrated at Nsukka and that the proposed Ogoja Campus should be a constituent College of the University.

ARCHITECTURE

The architectural plan of a University especially one that is in the process of reorganization and restructuring should be an integrated and flexible scheme appropriate to the academic design of the University. Thus the choice of predominant method of teaching (whether by lecture, Seminar or tutorial) will have special architectural effect. Since the buildings have got to express fundamental ideas about the nature of the University; the architectural programme demands the closest collaboration between architects, administrators and academics. It is, therefore, imperative that no effort should be spared in finding an architect of international distinction who is capable of resolving the academic, planning with student residence in architectural terms, who will seek through this design to satisfy the University's designer for a new relationship between the young and their teachers, between subjects and faculties and between contemplation and activity. The Council of this University, in deference to this philosophy, has appointed a firm, of architects of international repute, with extensive experience in University planning and building both in temperate and tropical countries, to design an architectural scheme which will conform to our academic organization.

Let me now turn to our academic planning. Both the academic and senior administrative staff are now actively addressing, themselves to the design of a new academic organization. The great question raised by the expansion of higher education are those of distribution of students, methods of teaching, appropriate curricula and staff-student relationship. To answer these questions it is proposed that the University of Nigeria should aim at being a Collegiate University. The plan is to have ultimately about 12 to 16 Colleges at Nsukka and about four to eight at Ogoja. Each College will contain 600 staff and students in the proportion of approximately 1:8 both men and women, and will have at its head a provost or master who is also a full-time member of the academic staff. The Colleges will differ from those of Oxford and Cambridge in that they will not be autonomous financially nor will they be responsible for admission of students or appointment of staff. They will differ from halls of residence of the civic university, the prototype of the University of Ibadan, in that teaching will be carried on in them and they will be self-governing enough to make their own rules. Every student will become a member of a College on admission to the University and may reside in that College. All staff will be members of Colleges and normally have working accommodation in them but will not reside in them. All Arts Faculty headquarters will be College-based. Science -Faculty headquarters may be-College-based or they may be placed within the respective Science Faculties. Teachers in Humanities and Social Studies will do their teaching in the College whilst those in Natural Sciences will do their teaching in the laboratory and in the facilities provided therein for teaching.

Colleges will contain junior and senior common rooms, a graduate common room, a reading room, a dining hall, a bar and a snack bar, academic staff offices, lecture halls and seminar rooms.The main purposes of the College system are:

1. To facilitate closer relationship between teacher and taught and so reduce if not completely remove, the mutual mistrust between staff and students which exists in our Universities and which leads to student unrest.

2. To provide valuable intimacies and loyalties of the life of a smaller community to a degree hardly possible if the unit is a whole large University.

3. To effect the intermingling of students following different courses of study and consequent widening of horizons.

4. To facilitate interchange between students of different Colleges as they attend seminars and tutorials held in other Colleges.

5. To improve teaching.

6. By centralising admission and the organization of teaching, the Collegiate scheme will recognise the importance of faculty or department as the focal point of the intellectual life of the University.

We cannot think of academic organization without at the same time considering the method of teaching best fitted for the type of organization we wish to adopt and which is most likely to achieve the desired close relationship between teacher and student which is one aspect of a deeper conception of University education. Of the known methods of teaching the tutorial in which the student meets his tutor at least once a week either alone or with one or two other students and Seminar or class discussion where the teaching is concentrated upon a group of about 8 to 15 students, are the best.

It will be our aim that the University of Nigeria should become an outstanding teaching and research University und we are, therefore, proposing, to adopt vigorous tutorial and seminar systems as the answer to the question of 'how to teach'.

The acceptance of the tutorial or seminar teaching as a fundamental element in the academic pattern will not preclude the recognition of the value of formal lecture involving large classes.

We recognise, however, that it is generally bad for students to go for long periods merely attending lectures or studying in isolation, without the face-to-face attention that tutorials and seminars provide. Only by such contact can students be led to see their studies in a wide context, be helped over their academic difficulties in good time and be encouraged to cultivate high scholarly standards for themselves. In our view, therefore, the tutorial and the seminar systems can and should be the most important part of what a young man or woman gets from our University and they are at their best the forms of instruction most closely related to individual needs and attainments than any other.

FACULTY ORGANIZATION:

It is our intention to retain to a very large extent the present Faculty organization with some modification.

The following Faculties, each headed by a Dean, are proposed:

(a) Faculty of Agriculture
(b) Faculty of Arts
(c) Faculty of Biological Sciences
(d) Faculty of Education
(e) Faculty of Engineering
(f) Faculty of Environmental Studies
(g) Faculty of Legal Studies
(h) Faculty of Medicine
(i) Faculty of Physical Sciences
(j) Faculty of Social Studies

It will be our aim to give the student the type of 'tertiary education' which will ensure that he is not only trained in his chosen speciality but also understands the basic characteristics, the modes of thought, of related disciplines, so that his spectrum of knowledge and understanding should be broad enough for him to emerge as an educated human being.

STUDENT AFFAIRS

I think it is generally agreed in the academic world that students should be closely associated with the work of the University as a whole, in key committees provided the students themselves show sense of responsibility and discipline, which is essential for the orderly deliberations and the understanding of the complex problems of universities in the modern world.

There is no doubt that a small minority of students do not care to be associated with this kind of participation and there is also a large majority of students who choose only to be drawn into University affairs at moments of special activity.

Nevertheless, we must make every effort to bring students directly into the mainstream of University life if they wish to be involved. Our main problem is to ensure that there is proper student representation not sectional representation but representation of the whole student body with which the University authorities could deal.

To this end, we propose that there should be a Student Representative Council, the S.R.C., representing student interests at the University level. In other words through the S.R.C. the student body will be represented in various University and Staff/Student committees. The S.R.C. will co-ordinate the activities of University clubs and societies, provide links with other institutions of learning and concern itself with all aspects of student welfare within the University. Its officers will be elected annually by a ballot of all students in the second term to serve for the following academic year. There will be a representative of each of the Colleges, the Athletic Union and the Alumni or Graduate Association and the S.R.C.

In addition, each faculty will elect four members to the S.R.C. except the Faculty of Engineering which will elect five members and the Faculty of Medicine which will elect six members. The number representing each faculty corresponds to the number of years of the course of study in the faculty. For example, the Faculty of Agriculture, which has four-year course of study will elect four members annually, one each for the first, second, third and fourth year students, respectively. All ordinary members of the S.R.C. will be elected annually shortly after the start of the academic year.

No officer of the S.R.C. will be eligible for re-election to the same office. No member of the S.R.C. will be elected for the third time. The President of the S.R.C. will be granted sabbatical leave from his studies without putting his academic career in jeopardy. The organisation of the S.R.C. allows students of all years to become involved in the running of student affairs.

Each College will have a Junior Common Room Committee which is concerned with the internal affairs of that College and the representation of student interest within the College. Sports Clubs will be affiliated to the Student Representative Council through the Athletic Union which will be jointly responsible with the Department of Physical Education for the co-ordination and promotion of Sport within the University.

General Meetings of the Student Body will be held at least twice every term. These meetings will have the sovereign right to decide S.R.C. and J.R.C. policy and to mandate S.R.C. or J.R.C. Committee on any issue. Representatives of the student body on various University and Staff/Student committees will also be accountable to the General Meeting. The General Meeting system ensures that every student has the opportunity to have a direct say in the running of student affairs and that important policy decisions are not taken by small committees in isolation. It is hoped that student participation in some aspects of the government of the University will be secured by the setting up of Staff/Student Committees empowered to discuss matters within the competence of Faculty Board except certain reserved items such as examination results, matters involving individual students or members of staff etc. One of the objects of this type of student organisation is to avoid the preposterous situation or near-anarchy that prevails in some Nigerian Universities.

It is my pleasant duty to acknowledge with gratitude our receipt of numerous benefactions which have come in since the reopening of the

University from Foundations, Charitable Organisations, Governments and individuals. To name all of them will lengthen this address and perhaps put unnecessary strain on your patience. I will, therefore, name only some of the benefactors and their gifts and will ask that those whom I have not mentioned will forgive me when I assure them that their gifts are just as much appreciated and valued as any other.

The following have been received:

1	From the Ford Foundation	a grant of £50,000 for students' textbooks
2	From the Ford Foundation	a grant of £50,000 for the purchase of Science equipment
3	From the British Government	a grant of £25,000 for re-equipping, the Libraries
4	From the British Government	a grant of £75,000 for the purchase of Science equipment
5	From the Royal Netherlands Government	A grant of £50,000 for the purchase of equipment in the Faculty of Engineering
6	From the Federal Republic of Germany	a grant of £5,000 for books in Physics und Chemistry
7	From the Federal Republic of Germany	a grant of £100,000 for equipment for the Departments of Chemistry and Physics
8	From the United States Agency for International Development (USAID)	A grant of £68,000 for the reconstruction of the C.E.C.
9	From USAID	A grant of £50,000 for the reconstruction of the Faculty of Agriculture Farm Centre Building
10	From the Ford Foundation	A grant of $110,000 for the reactivation of the Industrial Technical Education Programme

11	From AFPRINT Nigeria Ltd	A grant of £15,000 for the rehabilitation of the University
12	From UNICEF	A grant of £9,000 towards re-constructing the Department of Home Economics and two Volkswagen Kombi buses for the Department of Agricultural Economics
13	From theWorld Food Production	food items valued at a total of about £13,000 for feeding students
14	From Phillips (Nigeria) Ltd.	electronics equipment valued at £5,000
15	From the Government of the Midwestern State	750 students writing desks with matching chairs and a complete set of furniture for ten senior staff quarters
16	From the Government of Benue Plateau State	one Volkswagen mini bus
17	From the Joint University Council	books worth several thousands of pounds
18	From the Carnegie Corporation of New York	$10,000 for the packaging and shipping of books collected in the U.S.
19	From the Theological Education Fund, Bromley, Kent, England	about $8,000 towards an historical research scheme in the Department of Religion
20	From the World University Service Geneva	£1,000 for the establishment of a revolving loan fund for indigent students and several thousand pounds worth of medical equipment

21	From the Carnegie Corporation of New York	a grant of $.230,000 for the reactivation of the curriculum development and instructional materials resource centre for the Faculty of Education
22	From the Institute of Advanced Legal Education, London	about 5,000 items comprising books, pamphlets, periodicals, legislation and Law reports
23	From Ranfurly Library Services London	117 tea chests of books
24	From UNICEF	£1,600 for vacation employment of Agricultural Economics students

We thank our sister Universities of Ibadan, Ife, Ahmadu Bello and Lagos for the valuable assistance they gave us in various ways, especially in putting their facilities at the disposal of some of our final years students for practical courses.

I cannot conclude this address without directing my remarks to the graduands, the sixth group of men and women who represent this University's contribution to the manpower development of the country. For you the ceremony we now perform will bring special joy, in that in spite of your three years of academic inactivity, you were all able to satisfy the examiners that you are worthy of the degree, diploma and certificate of the University of Nigeria.

This is a remarkable achievement resulting from hard work often under conditions of indescribable hardship and privation. I congratulate you most heartily on your success. I hope that as you leave today to go into the world in various capacities you will always remember that you are amongst the fortunate few who have received the type of education that equips you to serve your people and your country. In the age of sophisticated materialism you will be exposed to all kinds of temptation the yielding to which may bring shame not only to yourselves and your loved ones but also to your *alma mater*. This University has endeavuored to inculcate in you the sense of honesty and integrity which should serve as a bulwark against forces of degradation and it is her constant prayer that you, her graduates, will at all times strive to live up to her ideals- the giving of selfless devoted and efficient service to your country.

I trust that on your part you will retain a keen interest in her affairs and be prepared, at all times, to make substantial contribution towards her development and progress. I would like to recommend to you the Alumni Association of this University. By identifying yourselves with the association you will gain an opportunity to participate in the affairs of the institution.

May I on behalf of the University say 'au revoir' and wish you well in your future endeavours.

Chapter 13

ADDRESS BY PROFESSOR H. C. KODILINYE, VICE-CHANCELLOR, UNIVERSITY OF NIGERIA, ON CONVOCATION DAY, DECEMBER 16, 1972

Your Excellency the Visitor, Your Highness the Chancellor, Pro-Chancellor, Your Excellency, My Lords, Distinguished Guests, Ladies and Gentlemen and Members of the University:

It is customary for the Vice-Chancellor to give an annual report on the state of his university at a Congregation on the Occasion of the Reception of Graduates. In pursuance of this tradition, I have the honour to present, in the form of an address, my report for the year ending December, 1972.

First of all, I would like to take this opportunity of welcoming all our guests to our Campus which, I am told by our aesthetically inclined friends, has one of the most picturesque sceneries in the country. Whilst you are with us, I hope you will find our climate most congenial and relaxing.

I should mention the appointment of our two Visitors, His Excellency, Dr. Ukpabi Asika, the Administrator of the East Central State and His Excellency, Brigadier U. J. Esuene, Military Governor of the South-Eastern State. The whole University is most grateful to His Excellency, the Head of State, General Yakubu Gowon, for doing us a great honour by appointing two illustrious sons of Nigeria, our own honorary graduates, to this high office of Visitation.

In the 16th century, Henry VIII's Chief Minister, Richard Cromwell, Earl of Essex, appointed Commissioners, Richard Layton and John London, to visit the University of Oxford. It was reported that the Visitors showed very little respect either for school men or for Monks as the undergraduates and their tutors were then respectively called. But they nevertheless made some provision for new teaching in Greek and Latin, in Medicine and in Civil Law. We shall hope that, during their visitations from time to time, our new Visitors will emulate the more generous of the two attitudes of the Tudor Oxford Visitors, in the interest of our welfare, our development and our progress. We shall look to them for guidance, understanding, inspiration and advice. We, on our part, do pledge to them our continued loyalty.

During the year, events of some significance took place. One of these, constituting an important development in our academic programme, is the decision of the Government of the East Central State to hand over the management of the Enugu Specialist Hospital to the University for a period of five years during which it is hoped the University will have built its own Teaching Hospital. This decision was in response to the request of the University Council to take over the management of the hospital in Order to provide the best possible facilities for medical education, for research and for efficient patient care. We shall devote our energy and skill to the training of our young men and women to become not only competent doctors but also good citizens imbued with the highest sense of service to their people and their country. I must here pay tribute to His Excellency, the Administrator of the East Central State, Dr. Ukpabi Asika, without whose foresight and magnanimity the taking over of the management of the hospital would not have been achieved. This University is most grateful to him for his support and encouragement and above all, for his confidence in us. We are mindful of the magnitude of the responsibility we have assumed in taking over the hospital but we can assure the Government of the East Central State that we will endeavour to reach and maintain our objectives in the interest of the nation.

We propose to establish a campus at Calabar and have been in negotiation with the Government of the South-Eastern State about this for some time now. The campus will be an extension of this University and will provide needed opportunity for university education for many of those young men and women, who, although they possess our entry qualifications, are unable to enter our portals here at Nsukka because of inadequate accommodation and facilities. We hope to start courses at the proposed campus early next session.

RECONSTRUCTION

In this area, very significant progress has been made. With the painting of students hostels and the re-installation of laboratory benches, the work of restoration of functional buildings should be regarded as complete. Repair of staff, houses, apart from painting which will soon be put in hand, is practically completed.

We have now embarked on the task of controlling the formidable Nsukka red earth. By tarring the principal roads on the campus, we hope to limit severely this menace.

Our swimming Pool has been fully restored after being out of commission for a period of five years. Its reactivation is a welcome augmentation of our recreational facilities. Our Stadium, which is another of the civil war casualties, is being reconstructed and should be brought back to full functional shape before the start of the West African University Games Zonal Competition due to take place later this month.

Apart from the Continuing Education Centre and the Home Economics buildings, whose rehabilitation was completed towards the end of 1971, significant additions have been made by the construction of permanent structures on the campus, particularly in the staff housing sector. By the end of this month, the building contractors are expected to hand over 30 residential units, 28 other units should be ready shortly after. This is not to be understood that we intend to provide campus residence for all our staff. What we have done is attempt to relieve the pressure of staff housing in the University caused by the effects of the civil war and also by the rural location of the University which precludes off-campus residence of suitable standard for renting by staff. We know that the cost of higher education continues to soar and that this places a heavy burden on the national purse which, in addition, has to provide the cost of national development in various other sectors. For this and other reasons, we agree that universities should husband their resources and insist on the judicious utilization of their revenue primarily for the purpose of imparting knowledge. We have, therefore, initiated negotiation with finance companies which we hope will lead to staff owning their houses either on university land or outside it. In this way, university funds will be used mainly to provide facilities for teaching, research and student care.

STAFF DEVELOPMENT AND TRAINING

The University reopened at the end of the war two years and nine months ago with severely depleted staff. Apart from the fact that the staff strength at the time stood at 279, just about a half of the staff numbers at the end of the 1966/67 session, the non-return of key academic staff at the end of hostilities deprived us of leadership in the various disciplines. Now I am happy to report that the position has changed dramatically. We now have in the service of the University staff of various nationalities numbering about 530. Confidence has returned and meaningful discussion has begun on the forward-planning schemes of the University to which I referred in my address last year.

We owe this improved staff situation to so many factors not the least of which is the co-operation of a number of foreign governments and charitable Foundations with whom we have technical aid arrangements. On behalf of the University I should express our gratitude especially to the Royal Netherlands, British, French and the Russian Governments, to the Universities of Oxford, Cambridge, Birmingham, Strathclyde, London, Dundee, Loughborough and Sussex for their co-operation in staff secondments. I should also wish to thank the Ford Foundation, British Voluntary Service Overseas, Canadian University Service Overseas and Canadian International Development Agency, in this regard. Most important, of course, is the enlightened policy of the Senate and Council which has resulted in the location and appointment of suitably qualified staff in all fields.

Quite early on my assumption of office, it was clear to me that the good name of the University would depend, among other things but perhaps more importantly, on the quality of its staff. Staff training and development therefore became the corner-stone of our policy. Every avenue is being explored to give staff of promise opportunities for further training and orientation. The result is that at the end of October this year, about 90 of our staff are on study leave for periods, ranging from three months to three years. They are spread through universities in Western Europe and North America; there are some also in Nigerian Universities. Additionally, over 30 members of staff have utilized available facilities to spend some spells in overseas universities in order to up-date themselves and renew acquaintance with colleagues and become conversant with improved methods in their disciplines.

Enlightened staff development programme enjoins that encouragement should be given to graduating students of promise who are keen on an academic career. The patient consideration of my Council of Deans has resulted in the formulation of the Junior Fellowship scheme whereby our own graduates with upper second honours degree or better are immediately absorbed into their relevant departments for twelve months in the first instance. If this early promise is borne out at the expiration of this period, the Fellows are enabled to proceed to higher degree courses for the next three years either in this University or in some other University recognized by Senate. At the moment some 47 Junior Fellows have been appointed. This programme is bound to strain our slender resources very severely, but it is about the only assured means of providing for a steady stream of trained men and women for academic positions in the University.

Staff development and training has not been restricted to the senior academic and administrative staff. Since the resumption, 30 junior and intermediate staff have gone on study leave in order to improve themselves. In-service-training has also been a steady and continuing process and has taken the form of seminars, colloquia and refresher courses.

The strengthening of the teaching staff has encouraged us to turn attention, as well, to the other important function of the University, which is research. Discussions of postgraduate programmes were interrupted by the war. Since the resumption of the University, the Department of Mathematics and Statistics and the Faculty of Education have been able to mount their postgraduate programme and have produced graduates with a Master's Degree. Under the directive of Senate the Postgraduate Studies Committee is exerting itself to produce further regulations, guidelines and programmes of postgraduate courses leading to the full range of higher degrees in the University. With this development most of the Junior Fellows should be able to undertake their advanced studies either fully here or in association with some other universities.

STUDENT AND GRADUATE NUMBERS

May I now turn to the more statistical aspect of this report in the Student Affairs Department?

(1)   The Present Figures: There are now 3,838 students, made up of 3,218 males and 620 females. Females constitute one-sixth of the whole.

(2)   In the 1966/67 session, the student population was 3,169, made up of 2,851 males and 312 females. Female students then constituted one-tenth of the student population.

   Deduction: Rise in student female population from one-tenth to one-sixth of the whole since 1967, excluding the war years.

(3)   The Student Population at resumption at the end of the war was 1,815.

   Deduction: The student population, inspite of various handicaps, has more than doubled itself within three years of the end of the war.

(4)   State Distribution of Students

   All the States of the Federation are represented in the student population thus reflecting the national outlook of the University.

True to its law, admission to the University is not determined by distinction as to race, religion, creed or tribal origin.

Graduates

(5) The total number of graduates of the University since inception is 3,467, of whom 298 are females. This is a significant contribution, inspite of the handicap of the recent sad episode, to manpower development in the country.

(6) Number of Graduates for this Session 758, of whom 74 are females. The University recorded nine first class honours degrees, the highest ever in any one year since the University began. There were also 96 second class honours upper division results. For the first time the Faculty of Education awarded higher degrees - the Masters degree in Education. There are five such graduates, one of whom is a woman.

BENEFACTIONS

In the past twelve months since I last addressed Convocation, we have continued to benefit from the goodwill of friends at home and abroad. These benefactions have ranged from the donation of a single title to the reactivation of a whole faculty. It is not my intention to name them all here - our gazette and other publications have given adequate coverage to these gifts and we have by individual direct communication sent our expressions of gratitude. To mention just a few, we have received the following benefactions:

1. British Council Enugu: Children's books (55 titles) to the University School.

2. Ford Foundation: Books(408 titles)

3. Professor R. W. French School of Business Administration & Professor G.B.Dox.see Department of History, Ohio University Athens Ohio, U.S.A. Books (229) titles)

4. C.U.S.o (Canadian University Service Overseas)
   Books (121 titles)

5. The Royal Society of London: Equipment worth £400 to Support work and the International Biological Programme.

6. Nigerian Universities Pensions Management Company Ltd. Lagos, 250 guineas for NUPEMCO PRIZE and Scholarship for the financial year 1971-72.

7. Kwara State Government: £1,000 towards the reconstruction of the University.

8. Midwestern State Government: One 55-seater passenger bus to the University. One Roneo Duplicator and one Typewriter for the Students Union.

9. Cavendish Laboratory,Cambridge: Laboratory equipment for the Department of Physics.

10. Department of Mathematics Brown University U.S A. Books (300 titles) to the Department of Mathematics/ Statistics.

11. Mrs. E. Aligekwe: Books (150 titles) to the Department of Mathematics/Statistics.

12. Corta, Aston House Dublin: £5,000 to cover the full costs (fees, travel and subsistence) of a graduate of this University in Animal Science to be trained in a University in Ireland.

13. Canadian Psychological Association: $2,,000 for the purchase of Tests and Equipment for the Department of Psychology.

14. Ford Foundation: $85,500 (reactivated grant) for the strengthening of the Economic Development Institute.

15. The Nigerian National Committee of the International Biological Programme: Equipment worth £250 to support work on the International Biological Programme.

Through bilateral aid agreements reached with the support of the Federal Government, we have collaborated with a number of foreign government agencies and foundations in our academic programmes. With the aid of the Carnegie Corporation of New York, work has resumed in the Faculty of Education on Curriculum Development leading to the establishment of the Curriculum Development and Instructional Materials Centre in which the Corporation is expected to invest the sum of $230,000 in six years. Population studies and demographic research has been reactivated with the grant of $230,000 from the Population Council to be spread over three years. In addition to staff secondment and training arrangements, the Canadian International Development_ Agency (CIDA) has undertaken to supply equipment over a four-year period in the area of agricultural engineering to the value of £130,000. Co-Operation with the Royal Netherlands Government which was inaugurated last session continues to bear fruit in the improved position of the Engineering Departments.

OUR GRADUATES

In this University we acknowledge the vocational interest of our students and seek to provide a training proper to their professional standards. We, therefore, hope that our graduates will go out with confidence into public employment or into private firms in the mixed economic system which exists in this country. But they are not conditioned by the University to accept the system without questioning its assumptions and methods. We believe in the progress which comes by asking questions and in the independence of mind which faces difficult issues. The graduates who lazily relapse into the set habit of "organisation men" and run away from many questions which need to be answered about our social and economic system, are our failures, not our successes. We offer vocational courses in the spirit of encouraging a fundamental curiosity and a habit of thought which does not avoid the difficult questions. A great many of our students come to us to continue a general education of the mind and a development of specific abilities without any precise vocational intentions. We seek with them also to encourage a questioning attitude;

though it is sometimes necessary to remind people that asking awkward questions without answering them is a negative process and that we look also for an ability in constructive thought. As a University we should neither be vocational nor anti-vocational in bias: we should simply note that the motivation of some students is strengthened by these vocational intentions and that we should use our common-sense to prepare them, as well as we can, for the work they wish to do.

Universities are given a considerable measure of autonomy because of the need to protect the freedom of speculative thought, which can be the source of important and unforseen advances. What we should or should not teach or how we teach or what should be the subject of research must remain our responsibility. But this does not mean that we should shut ourselves off from the community and ignore its ideas and suggestions, which will often be helpful and relevant. The outside interests must be given an assurance that they will be heard and their ideas seriously considered. They must be given opportunity for dialogue with the academic community, while accepting the ultimate right of the free scholar to go his own way, however unpopular. In most universities of the Western World the freedom of the academic community is expressed in the dominance of Senate over all academic matters. The convention that Senate should not be over-ruled on these matters is a further expression of the importance given to the protection of freedom of thought.

OBITUARY

Since the last convocation we have lost by death from a motor accident one member of the academic staff and one student. Dr. Jamie Brooks seconded to this University under the Canadian University Service Overseas Scheme died on Good Friday as a result of the injuries she received in a motor accident. Mr. Vincent Ubanwa, a student in the Faculty of Agricultural Sciences also met his death in the same accident. Another student, Mr Samuel Babatunde Ande, in the Faculty of Social Sciences died from natural causes at Enugu Specialist Hospital only a day before Miss Brooks. Miss Brooks and Mr. Ande were given a fitting burial at the University cemetery. We also lost Mr.Ezenyeaku who was Assistant Dean of Student affairs, Miss Bessie Okoye who would have graduated along with others today in Fine Arts, Mr. Emmanuel Ogbuabor, a student in the Faculty of Business Administration, Mr.Archibong Nkanta, a student in the Faculty of Agricultural Sciences and Mr Samuel Elike., Faculty of Science. Seven members of the junior staff also died during the period -Mrs. M. U. M Amadi, Mrs. Comfort Chibuzor, Messrs. B.Obelly, Lawrence Eze, B. A. Ise and Omeje Okoro. Last but not the least we lost Professor Eyo Ita, our revered honorary graduate.

Miss Brooks' parents have recently sent to the University a cup to be competed for at the Inter-University Games of the Nigerian Universies Games Association. In addition, a scholarship for graduate studies in Statistics has been offered to the University by the Canadian University Service Overseas. The University is acknowledging these benefactions with gratitude.

Finally, I wish to congratulate the graduands for the successful completion of their courses and the prize winners for their achievement. Those who are leaving us will carry with them the best wishes of this University in whatever their future careers may be. We hope that they will uphold her good name and be a living testimony of her endeavours to train and educate the youth for the service of their country and peoples. You will be expected to eschew all false doctrines, to maintain the highest integrity, to abhore prejudices whether on religious, racial or ethnic grounds, to defend and protect the weak, and to be just in all your dealings with your fellow men and women. I recommend to you the Alumni Association of the University. You should join and become active members for by so doing you will be in a better position to serve the interest of your *Alma Mater*.

PROFESSOR H C KODILINYE VICE-CHANCELLOR

OFFICE OF THE VICE-CHANCELLOR

DATE: DECEMBER 16, 1972.

Chapter 14

ADDRESS TO CONGREGATION BY THE VICE-CHANCELLOR, PROFESSOR KODILINYE ON JULY 1973

Members of Congregation, during the last meeting of Congregation, which was the first since I became the Vice-Chancellor of the University, I spoke briefly on different issues touching this community. I also shared with you the faith in the future greatness of the institution and the nation it serves, which made me accept the invitation to take up the onerous burden of being Vice-Chancellor here. On that occasion, I spoke rather informally and from notes. To be sure I came with certain visions, certain hopes and plans, but it was necessary to match those against the hard realities of a university just emerging from a terrible trauma before committing them to permanent record.

On this occasion, it is different. I have worked with and amongst you since April 1971. During this period, I have succeeded in testing my ideas and formulations and in working out an integrated plan for rebuilding and developing the University. It is on this that I want to speak to you this morning with the single aim of having briefed you on the condition of the University as it passes over to the Federal Military Government. This is necessary in order to enable you to participate meaningfully and constructively in the process of debate and action by which a University, adequately equipped to fulfil its assigned role in a rapidly changing nation like ours, will emerge.

Physical Development: There are two sides to this matter. The first is the rehabilitation of the University to its pre-civil war condition. The second concerns the fundamental re-structuring of the institution with reference to its physical layout, teaching programmes and methods, orientation, and social relationships in order to pull it up to a level where it can compete favourably with the best of its kind and produce a breed of men and women who will be the pride of their country.

With regard to reconstruction and rehabilitation we have come a long way from 1970 and I doubt that it is necessary, or even possible, to enumerate here all the facilities which have been brought to their pre-war standard or nearly so. But a few stand out prominently. These include the Continuing Education Centre, the Home Economics building, the University swimming pool and Stadium, classroom and laboratory fixtures, furniture for staff houses, students hostels, the Medical Centre, the University Bookshop Limited and our major roads.

In a few areas we have even surpassed pre-civil war standards. There are now many more houses for senior staff - 334 at Nsukka and 45 at Enugu. If we add those for Junior and Intermediate Staff (69 in number), that gives us a total of 448 residential units. In laboratory and office space, we are also better provided than we were in 1966 through the construction of prefabricated buildings. In respect of the old staff houses, the main remaining repair work is painting which has already started in earnest. If the contractors keep to their schedule, it is expected that all the old houses will wear a new and refreshing look by the next Convocation in December this year. Similarly the transport section of the Works Department now has many more cars than in 1971. In this area we have even found it possible to provide some Faculties, Institutes and other Units with demonstrable need for them, with cars and Land Rovers.

This is not to pretend that we have attained the stage in our rehabilitation programme where we can afford to rest on our oars. We are still not able to house all our staff. For instance, while we have accommodation for 379 senior staff, our present senior staff establishment stands at 505. Also, although we have increased classroom and laboratory space, we are still unable to mount or assemble vital scientific equipments, some of which therefore are yet lying in the packages in which they arrived. But the point I am making is that the administration has not been idle or insensitive to our crying needs. We have made every effort to advance at a rate commensurate with our very limited resources in money and trained hands.

It is interesting to note that my colleague, the Vice-Chancellor of our sister University of Ahmadu Bello, in his convocation address of 2nd December, 1972, stated as follows:-

'Those who feel that University students are coddled should see how our first year students fit in four to a room. Similarly, the other University facilities-classrooms, reading space and recreational facilities - are over-strained. University staff have been housed in caravans, and we provide no housing for our junior staff members. Students and staff have borne a difficult situation with patience. Some of the building facilities are due to lack of money. But others are due to a sheer lack of building capacity in this area'

Yet, in 1972, Ahmadu Bello University's recurrent expenditure was well over £10 million and her capital estimate was about £5.8 million. Our own recurrent estimate for 1971-72 was £3,872,280, of which we received only £1,930,303, leaving a deficit of £1,941,977. This indicates the magnitude of our financial embarrassment.

However, you will be glad to know that I am now in a position to submit a memorandum to Council praying that off-campus allowance to staff should be increased to £30 (N60.00) per month and that staff should be allowed yearly leave allowance, that is for both local and vacation leaves.

In the area of development, defined as the re-structuring of the University in the light of the needs and tempo of today, which are radically different from the 1960s, we have succeeded in working out a master-plan for implementation as soon as the necessary funds are available. In fact, we have gone further and translated our ideas for the University into architectural design which takes account of both physical beauty and utility.

The basic principles of the new development plan are already known to all. They are embodied in my blueprint which has been discussed and debated at all levels of the decision-making process of this University - Departmental and Faculty Boards, the Development Committee, Senate Council. In sum, the new plan aims to improve the quality of teaching and the frequency of contact between staff and students by de-emphasising instruction through lectures while emphasising the seminar and tutorial system. By bridging the social gap between staff and students, it seeks to remove alienation amongst students and, therefore, to minimise unrest. And finally, by taking physical beauty into account, the new approach will give the University what it presently lacks –elegance and majesty.

There are other aspects of the physical development of the University which deserve mention here. First, there is the Calabar Campus of the university which is scheduled to start teaching in October this year. The origin of the idea of a campus of this University in the South-Eastern State is too well known to demand recapitulation here. A permanent site for the campus has now been chosen on the banks of the Great Kwa River. But, to begin with, the campus will have a temporary home at Duke Town Secondary School which is already being reconditioned for that purpose. The Deputy Registrar, Mr O.A.Ufot, has been deployed to oversee arrangements. A Board of Management has also been constituted comprising the Vice-Chancellor (Chairman), the Principal, Calabar campus, the Deans of the Faculties, three members of Senate, the Registrar, the Bursar and the Librarian, with the Deputy Registrar as Secretary. An Acting Principal has been appointed in the person of Professor D.B.U.Ekong, a distinguished academic who also holds the substantive position of Professor of Chemistry at this University.

Maybe I should mention here that we are not building a new University at Calabar, but merely a campus of this University. This means that the academic programme of that campus will be determined and controlled by the University of Nigeria Senate, and its policy and other relevant matters by the University Council.

The second physical project also requiring mention here is the University of Nigeria Teaching Hospital (UNTH). As it has not been possible, owing to financial and other constraints, to start the building of a teaching hospital immediately, the University of Nigeria authorities approached the Government of the East Central State, which kindly agreed to hand over its former specialist Hospital at Enugu, for our use as a teaching hospital for a period of five years. The hospital is already operating as such. The process of screening the staff to make sure that each of those absorbed has the minimum requirement at his/her own level for holding a position at such an institution has been completed.

The University Council has constituted a Board of Governors for the Hospital, made up of the Vice-Chancellor as Chairman, representatives of the Council, representatives of Senate, the Permanent Secretary, ministry of Health and Social Welfare, Enugu, representatives of the Nigeria Medical Association and of the Medical Advisory Committee of the Teaching Hospital. The Registrar is the Secretary to this Board.

And thirdly, there is the question of student numbers as an aspect of physical growth. Under the master-plan for the expansion of the university in the eight-year period 1072-1980, we are committed to attaining a student population of 10,000 in the early 1980s. This would represent an increase of well over 6,000 students on the present strength of 3,838. Out of this number, about 1,000 will be pursuing postgraduate courses.

These are prodigious commitments requiring the expenditure of about 63.2 Naira. We are committed to the programme because it is the only way to ensure that the conditions of work at the university and its graduates maintain standards comparable to those in other reputable universities in the world. It is also necessary as a means of raising the morale and productivity of our staff who have all along, even before the war brought its own destruction, worked under severe deprivation and handicap.

Staff Development and Conditions of Work: I now come to staff development and conditions of work. The realisation of the ends set forth in our master-plan for development depends first an foremost on the ability of well trained, competent, hardworking and dedicated staff, academic and administrative, senior and junior. This has been clear to me from the beginning and is the explanation for the staff development plan which I have pursued since my assumption of office. There are many aspects to this question of staff development and conditions of work. They include staff recruitment, training, work conditions appraisal and promotions. I shall briefly discus the principles guiding my approach to each of these aspects and the progress we have made in each case.

Staff recruitment in universities is normally based on demonstrated ability and never on race creed or colour. The result is that a university is usually a microcosm in terms of the racial composition of its staff and students. This ensures that the University is exposed to as many ideas and points of view as possible and that its life is lifted above local divisive issues. Because of the sad experience of their recent past the new African nations are, however, anxious to ensure that, while their Universities are international in the above sense, the determination of policy and objectives is in their own hands. It is to this end that overall University policy is usually in the hands of a Council comprising responsible citizens. Effort is always made to ensure that the majority of the teaching and administrative staff are indigenes, many of whom should hold responsible positions as Deans, Heads of Departments and Directors of Research Institutes.

There were in 1967 about 400 senior staff in the service of the University. Of these, 75% were Nigerian, and 25% expatriate. On resumption at the end of the war, only about 60% of the pre-war staff strength reported for duty; and all of them were Nigerian. To recoup the University's losses in this area and give its staff establishment the international character it requires for a dynamic and fruitful existence, a vigorous staff recruitment policy was pursued in which both indigene and expatriates were offered appointment, if found suitable. As a result, by 1971/72 the senior staff strength had risen to 455, of which 70 were administrative and 385 academic. Of a total strength of 455, 419 were Nigerian and 36 expatriate. At this stage the percentage of expatriates to Nigerians stood at 6.78%. As of June 30 1973, the strength of the senior staff of the University stood at 565, of which 63 were expatriate, that is, the latter constitute 11.15% of the total. Thus as of now, the proportion of our expatriate colleagues and friends stands at 13.75% below the pre-civil war level.

In the 1972/3 session, no expatriate was a Dean of Faculty. Of the 55 Heads of Department and Units, 46 were Nigerian and 9 expatriate. Of the 50 Readers and Professors, 38 are Nigerian and 12 expatriate. These figures for expatriates are well below pre-civil war figures and far behind the figures for expatriates in our sister Nigerian universities. With regard to staff recruitment, therefore, I have given every encouragement to qualified indigenous staff. We, like other Universities, have recognised that few nations have all the men to staff their Universities. I have mentioned these figures only to put the record right because a good deal of misinformation has been propagated by some quarters for reasons only known to themselves.

As mentioned above, another important aspect of staff development is training. The civil war compelled those of our staff who were caught on this side of the Niger to engage themselves for thirty months, in other than academic work. Consequently, at the end of the war, our academics were indeed very rusty in a world where knowledge grows every minute. It was to enable them to update themselves and renew contacts in other parts of the world that we have pursued a liberal policy enabling staff to go on study leave for periods varying from 3 months to three years. At this moment, we have about 100 of our staff abroad on study leave. This figure is higher than that of any other University.

Another aspect of our staff training and development policy deals with the recruitment of promising young Nigerians whom we keep for one year as Junior Fellows. They are then sent away to pursue graduate studies in their different fields. This programme enables us to control the training of these young men and women according to a rationale determined by their competence and the needs of the University and the country. As of June 30 1973, there were 55 of these Junior Fellows in the service of the University. We have not only found schools for those of them who have completed their mandatory service but also guaranteed their maintenance during the years of their training. We hope that in the next few years, our dependence on the outside world for university staff will be further reduced. There is no other University in Nigeria which has such a comprehensive scheme of staff development.

It remains to mention, in this connection, our programme for post-graduate work, which, in a sense, is an aspect of our staff development policy. It is usually the ambition of any university to provide facilities for the further training of the more promising students in the techniques of the search for knowledge. Some of these it employs to meet its own needs, the others it puts into the labour market to be absorbed by other universities or by other sectors of the nation's economy. The University of Nigeria is naturally anxious to start its own graduate training programme, or more correctly, to expand it since the Departments of Education, Mathematics and Political Science are already doing something in this regard. The Senate postgraduate Committee, the Faculties and the Departments have worked out the relevant Regulations. Advertisements have gone out in various areas and to next sessions destined to mark a new beginning in the academic programme of the University. With this, I am sure, the problems of training our young men and women for their future work in this and other universities will be further reduced.

And now I come to the issue of staff appraisals and promotions, which is the subject of intense interest. Staff morale depends not only on good training and adequate facilities but even more on adequate reward for good work. The emphasis is on <u>reward for good work</u>. In the early years of this, as of any other university, when the main concern was to get started, and the easiest way to start was to concentrate on teaching, reward or promotion for good work meant promotion for good teaching and loyal service on those university committees which service teaching. But by 1966, the University, like other universities which have established teaching, had come to recognise that the University work did not just mean teaching and service to the community, but also contribution to knowledge and was starting to base assessment and promotions on these three criteria.

To my mind, it is useless to debate whether teaching is more important or more onerous than research or vice-versa. The accomplished university man is the one at home in both fields and who is, therefore, able to let his research fertilise his teaching. Which in its turn helps to suggest problems for investigation. This is not to say that all university teachers must be accomplished in the above sense, for there are some who are more at home in one than the other. The point, nevertheless, is that the rate of advancement or promotion varies, in the best tradition of universities, according to the individual's approximation to that ideal of excellence in teaching and research. Any university which forever ignores this fact in favour of some other less tested criteria is doomed to mediocrity.

On paper, the above principle sounds rather rigid, and some would say unfair. But in practice, each university applies it, bearing in mind its own peculiar circumstances. This, at least, has been the case with us here. Inspite of the insistence that our academic staff must now, like their colleagues elsewhere, become conscious of research and publication, as the handmaid of good teaching, our promotions policy has been fairly liberal, even up to the Readership level which should normally not be the case. As a result, the statistics of promotion since the end of the war is quite impressive, in fact, at times out of all proportion to the number of people who have actually sought to put this University on the world map of scholarship by means of their publications. The following benefitted from the promotions exercise:-

From 1st July, 1970	46
From 1st July, 1971	38
From 1st July, 1972	3
From 1st July 1973	37

Of these, 10 were promoted Professors, 18 to Readerships and 53 to Senior Lectureships.

These figures are very high, bearing in mind that not all members of staff are due for assessment every year, and that not all those theoretically due for assessment would meet the minimum require-ments for promotion. But, no matter how much one sugar-coats the basic principle that should guide promotions in universities, nobody should be in any doubt about the fact that we have entered a new era in which good teaching must be buttressed with good research.

The argument has often been that conditions in the University do not encourage research. There is no doubt that our libraries and laboratories are not in all respects as good as some of the best in Africa. Nor are our offices and houses air-conditioned and cosily furnished. To concede this however, is not to say that we are in such a state of under-development as to warrant absolute inactivity in any of the two main facets of the university teachers' duties. In any case, the whole effort towards rehabilitation and reconstruction is aimed at improving these conditions. I doubt that anyone can seriously contend that we should do nothing until the optimum condition is reached in library and laboratory condition.

Still, we have done what is possible to improve staff living conditions. I have already mentioned the rehabilitation and reconstruction of staff houses and offices, the supply of improved furniture and the grant of study leave and tours. Maybe I should also mention here the fact that we have succeeded in obtaining some money to enable staff to purchase vehicles so that they can be easily mobile in the interest of their work – teaching and research. As of June 30 1973, the University had granted loans amounting to about a million ₦aira to 317 staff for the purchase of cars. By the same date, about ₦500,000.00 had been made available to the junior staff for the purchase of motor- cycles.

Contact with outside bodies: Though we have not gone cap in hand to beg for help and relief, many noble- minded individuals, philanthropic bodies, institutions and foreign governments have come to our aid with a rich assortment of help. On the question of staff training and recruitment, we have established technical assistance arrangements with, among others, the Royal Netherlands, British, French and Russian governments, the Universities of Oxford, Cambridge, Birmingham, Strathclyde, Dundee, Loughborough and Sussex; the British Voluntary Service Overseas, the Canadian Voluntary Service Overseas, Canadian International Development Agency, the Ford Foundation and the Rockefeller Foundation.

Federal Take-over: And now I come to an issue in which all of us are keenly interested. As we all know, the University was reopened in 1970 as a joint venture between the Governments of the East Central and South Eastern States on the one hand and the Federal Military Government on the other. Under this arrangement, the two State governments were, between them, to take responsibility for 70% of our recurrent budget, while the Federal Government was to take care of the remaining 30%. In spite of their heroic efforts, the East Central and South Eastern States were quite unable to meet their financial commitments to the University. In the event, we found ourselves operating a very light budget mainly on the basis of the 30% Federal subvention. Efforts to get the Federal Military Government to extend to us the same treatment as was meted out to Ahmadu Bello University, 75% of whose recurrent budget was paid for by that government failed.

Now I am happy to report that the Federal Military Government has magnanimously decided to take over the University. One of the implications of this is that the Federal Military Government will now underwrite our entire budget. We can thus say that our financial crisis is about to be over. The effective date of takeover is, I believe April 1, 1973.

I wish to take this opportunity to thank their Excellencies, Dr Ukpabi Asika, and Brigadier U.J.Esuene and their governments for the part they played in reactivating the University and enabling it to operate until the Federal Military Government stepped in. We are also grateful to His Excellency, the Head of State and Commander-in-Chief of the Armed

Forces, General Yakubu Gowon, and his Government for the decision to convert the University of Nigeria into a Federal University.

The Federal take-over of the University implies for us immense advantages and even graver responsibilities. More than before we need all hands on deck to discharge these responsibilities to the satisfaction of our friends, well-wishers and the Nigerian peoples. It is my conviction that you are all committed to the great ideas for which this University stands and that you will spare no efforts to co-operate with me in the pursuit of those ideas and in the discharge of our new responsibilities.

Thank you.

H.C. Kodilinye

Vice-Chancellor

Office of the Vice-Chancellor

University of Nigeria

Nsukka 7 July 1973

Chapter 15

AN ADDRESS BY THE VICE CHANCELLOR, PROFESSSOR H. C. KODILINYE, ON THE OCCASION OF THE SECOND MATRICULATION CEREMONY HELD AT THE UNIVERSITY OF NIGERIA, NSUKKA CAMPUS, SATURDAY, NOVEMBER 3, 1973

Members of the Council of Deans, Members of Senate, Heads of Administrative Units, other members of senior staff, my students, Ladies and Gentlemen.

It is my great pleasure to preside over this very important ceremony of matriculation by which those who have recently been accepted to undergo full-time courses in this University are formally admitted into membership of the University. This ceremony, although recently introduced, has become institutionalized as an essential element in our academic calendar. As a University we have a short history, but as we grow in age we acquire new traditions to enrich existing ones.

'Incertum est quam longa_nostrum cuiusque vita
futura sit, sed traditiones in aeternum florebunt,
nulla academic sine his stare potest.'
It is uncertain how long the life of each one of us will be,
But traditions will live forever, and
no university can be stable without them.

Our innovations in this University have always been efforts at combining reconstruction with restructuring, thus crystalizing the goals of the University. By and large, these efforts are in consonance with the traditions of the great universities of the ancient and western worlds. The matriculation exercise is, therefore, a process of identification with and enrolment in the University, an act of formal admission of students into the University in statu pupillapi.

At this ceremony, the University prescribes an oath to which the students must subscribe in fulfillment of an act of commitment to the philosophy of the University of Nigeria. By signing the matriculation register, the student accepts all the rights and privileges of the members of the University as well as the obligations and responsibilities of that membership.

As a matter of fact, every institution selects or rejects its members in accordance with a wide variety of formal rules and informal codes. Your admission has been guided by the law establishing this University. A significant section of this law requires that every matriculant should not be below the age of 17, at which age one is expected to have achieved some degree of maturity and be ready to discard specific childhood roles and assume a wide range of adult roles. It is, therefore, expected that as you vow before your Vice-Chancellor to accept your new roles as students of this University, you are fully aware of the implications of any violation of such vows.

Competition for admission this year has been the keenest ever in the history of this University. Last year for example, a little less than 7,000 candidates qualified to sit the entrance examination and 3,926 qualified to be considered for direct entry. This year 12,995 candidates qualified to sit the entrance examination and 4,562 were considered for direct entry. Of the total figure of 17,55 persons who applied for admission, 16,601 qualified for consideration but only 1,431 were finally selected. You belong to this fortunate few. The number of applications for transfers from other universities to this University has also increased by 6.58%.

By your registration you are certified to be in possession of all the requirements as to maturity as attested by your age, as to academic requirements and as to character as demonstrated in the testimonials from your principals or former employers.

On the firm conviction that you are capable adults, it is my considered view that you should be accorded responsible roles in running the affairs of this University. Accordingly we must discard the old concept of a university as a society of master and disciples, societas magistrorum et discipulorum, which has led to the existence of a gap and some suspicion between staff and students. This University accepts you into this community of scholars, «universitas scholalium», and, therefore, expects your full participation in the urgent task of bridging the gap between staff and students.

Within the past three years, this gap has visibly narrowed down. In order finally to bridge it a scheme has been devised whereby junior members of the University, as matriculated students, will through the students Representative Council, participate in staff-student dialogue in matters within the competence of the faculty boards with the exception of specific items such as examinations, staff matters and the general security of the University. This is an opportunity that does not exist anywhere else in Nigeria and I am once again calling on the Students Union officials and the Dean of Student Affairs office to set up the necessary machinery for restructuring of the Students Representative Council along the lines outlined in my speech at the matriculation ceremony last year.

This is an honest attempt to ensure that the growing concern about the alienation of students in some other institutions does not spread to this healthy place. That is why I am resolved that in the restructuring of this University as a proper academic community, due emphasis should be placed on personal attention, humane education and direct interaction between staff and students.

An Address by the Vice-Chancellor

ACADEMIC DRESS

Last year, we were able to introduce the wearing of academic dress. This was in fulfillment of a long standing request in 1960/61 by the first executive of the University of Nigeria Students Union. It is significant to note that it took 12 years to meet this request.

To emphasize the importance of academic dress, it has been decided that it should be worn by students on the following occasions:

1. when appearing before the Vice-Chancellor;

2. at University ceremonies, including Convocation, Matriculation, and at University sermons;

3. at University examinations.

My experience with last year's matriculating group gives me much confidence in the ability of my students to honour their matriculation vows and wear the academic dress with pride and dignity.

I must end this short address by expressing the hope that you will derive, during your stay with us, all the inspiration, guidance and happiness which this great institution offers within its portals.

H. C. Kodilinye, Vice-Chancellor.

Office of the Vice-Chancellor, University of Nigeria,

Nsukka.

November 3 1973

UNIVERSITY OF NIGERIA

AN ADDRESS BY THE VICE-CHANCELLOR, PROFESSOR H. C. KODILINYE GIVEN AT THE UNIVERSITY OF NIGERIA, NSUKKA, ON CONVOCATION DAY, DECEMBER 15TH 1973

Your Excellency, General Yakubu Gowon, Head of the Federal Military Government and Commander-in-Chief of the Armed Forces, the Honourable Chief Justice of the Federation, Your Excellencies the Administrator of the East Central State and the Military Governors, Your Highness the Emir of Kano and Chancellor of the University, the Pro-Chancellor, My Lords Spiritual and Temporal, Distinguished Guests, Members of the University:

It is with great pleasure that I welcome you all to this Convocation for the conferment of degrees, the ninth in the history of this University. This is the second time this year that we have had the opportunity of playing host to such a galaxy of distinguished guests. Just last August, we were honoured with a visit by two of Africa's most illustrious sons - His Excellency Gaafar El Nemiery, the President of the Republic of the Sudan and His Excellency General Yakubu Gowon, our own Head of State. We of this University fondly remember how at the conclusion of that day's activities, our Head of State, in a brief and captivating farewell remark, promised to be here again soon. We are deeply grateful to him that in spite of the pressure of other equally important engagements, he has found the time to be with us today.

It is customary on an occasion such as this, for the Vice-Chancellor to brief Congregation, at conferment of degrees, on the work which the University has been doing.

In the convocation address of 1971, I traced briefly the history of the University in order to remind ourselves of the high ideals and principles which the founders sought to realise through the establishment of this institution. I described the severe physical, intellectual and moral damages which the regrettable events of 1967-1970 inflicted on the University. After openly proclaiming our re-dedication to the ideals of our founders, I promised to do my best not only to restore the institution to its pre-civil war standing, but to take it to even greater heights of achievement.

The 1972 Convocation address carried the story of not inconsiderable progress in reconstruction and rehabilitation inspite of our very slender resources. That we achieved as much as we did then, was made possible by the paternal understanding of the Federal Military Government and of the Governments of the East Central and South-Eastern States, by the generosity of friends, well-wishers and philanthropic individuals and bodies from within and without this country and by the dedication, mutual loyalty and cooperation of my staff and students.

My address this year is about even more noteworthy successes in making this University worthy of its name and of the great nation which it serves. In many respects this year's Convocation is a remarkable one. It is the third since I assumed the office of Vice-Chancellor in this University. It is the first which we are holding as a Federal institution. And what is more we have here today as a special guest of honour one of Nigeria's, and indeed Africa's most famous sons - the honest and gentle General Yakubu Gowon whose firmness saved this nation in its hour of greatest peril.

An occasion as momentous as this would deserve a marathon address detailing our successes and difficulties in the past three years. But precisely because it is so momentous, we have a very crowded programme. For this reason, therefore, I shall be very brief in high-lighting the main events in our recent history by focusing mainly on the way we have grown physically and academically in the process of living up to our duty of service to Nigeria.

RECONSTRUCTION AND PHYSICAL GROWTH

In this aspect of our history the first point worthy of mention is the fact that we can now proudly claim to have completed (with the single exception of the Princess Alexandra Auditorium) the work of post-war reconstruction. Those who, since the end of the civil war, are visiting us for the first time today may not fully understand what we here mean by reconstruction or appreciate the extent to which it has absorbed our time and resources since 1970. At the end of the civil war the then two campuses of the University wore a most desolate and dilapidated look. The buildings were stripped of louvres, doors, tiles and of all furnishings - a few had even been burnt down. The laboratories were bare of equipment while the holdings of our libraries were badly depleted - losses totalling in the case of the Nsukka Campus Library over 40% of total stock. The roads were damaged and the lawns over-grown. The result was that when I came here in 1971, that is after a year or so of dogged attempts to rebuild, I met my staff and students still living in shutterless, doorless and unfurnished houses, teaching and reading in classrooms, libraries and laboratories that were hardly equipped. Those were the days when my students used their legs to support their lecture notes in the absence of chairs and benches.

But today the story is entirely different, it is a happy one. We have in most cases attained the pre-civil war condition, while in a few areas we have even surpassed it. Both the Student hostels and staff houses have been repaired, re-equipped and repainted. For about six months now they have worn a refreshing and cheering look. The laboratories, libraries and lecture rooms have been restocked. In fact in the case of some Departments - such as Physics and Chemistry - we have attained conditions which are not only better than what we had in 1967 but which will excite the envy of some of their best stocked counterparts in black Africa. In the case of the Library we have added since 1970, 40,577 volumes to our holdings.

Improvements in our physical layout have not been limited to the reconstruction and rehabilitation of the pre-war structures. We have gone further to add new structures made absolutely necessary by our increased intake of students and by our growth in other directions. Thus with regard to staff accommodation we have completed 40 new bungalows, three blocks of flats each capable of providing accommodation for six families, and a police post with houses for policemen. In order to meet the demand for more office, laboratory and workshop space, we have provided extra structures for the following Departments and Units:

Medical Centre
Student Affairs
Pharmacy
Biochemistry
Microbiology
Physics
Animal Science
Botany
Fine and Applied Arts
The Social Sciences
Faculty of Education
Faculty of Agricultural Sciences
The University Primary School

We also have at an advanced stage of construction, 25 staff bungalows, two blocks of six flats each, a slaughter house, an extension for the Department of Pharmacy and a fence to improve the security of the Nsukka campus.

Many of these additions, as those of you who have toured the campus would have seen, are temporary structures erected to deal with a situation which has reached a stage of emergency. They must not be considered as the final solution to our problems of accommodation and equipment. Through the support and encouragement of the Federal Government and the National Universities Commission, we have produced a master plan for rebuilding the University in such a way that it will be a source of pride to this nation and also to all who are associated with the University in any way.

Nor has physical growth been limited to the erection of new structures or the extension of old ones. It has also meant for us increase in the number of academic units in which we organise teaching and research. Whereas formerly we had nine faculties, now we have eleven with the creation of the Faculty of Environmental Studies and the reorganisation of what was formerly the Faculty of Science into the two Faculties of Physical and Biological Sciences. There has also been an increase in the number of departments with the creation of the new department of Paediatrics in the Faculty of Medicine. Whereas formerly we had only four units devoted to research, we now have six with the creation of Curriculum Development and Instructional Materials Centre and the Demographie Centre.

Two other aspects of our physical growth deserve special mention here. One is the University of Nigeria Teaching Hospital (UNTH). Owing to severe financial and other constraints we were unable to undertake the building of a Teaching Hospital as soon as we needed one. Instead we approached the Government of the East Central State which very generously agreed to our use of the former Enugu Specialist Hospital for a period of five years. I am happy to report that the Hospital is now functioning as such under a Board of Governors constituted by the University of Nigeria Governing Council. We maintain that this arrangement is the best way to ensure that adequate facilities and expertise which only the University can provide are available for the training of our young men and women to become not only competent doctors but also good citizens. To disturb this arrangement and adopt the archaic policy being pursued in similar institutions will not only be disastrous for medical education but will put in jeopardy the standard of medical care so far achieved. Today in Britain there is increasing realisation that medical science has become so complex that the control of Teaching Hospitals must inevitably pass to the Universities.

The other remaining important development in the area of physical growth is the establishment of a campus of this University at Calabar, the headquarters of the South-Eastern State. Again owing to limited resources the campus started with a temporary home at the Duke Town Secondary School. The Universty Council, taking into account the special problems of this campus and its distance from the parent campus, constituted a Board of Management to supervise its growth. An Acting Principal has been appointed in the person of Professor D.E.U. Ekong who holds the substantive position of Professor of Chemistry at this University. On October 5 last, 162 students registered for courses at the Calabar Campus in the following areas: English, History, Geography, Sociology, Botany, Zoology, Chemistry, Physics and Mathematics.

As I said earlier on, the creation of new units and the erection of new structures have been made necessary by increased student enrolment and staff intake. In short much of what we have done, we have done out of a desire to meet our obligations to the people and the nation. On October 1, 1970, we had a student enrolment of 2,934. But by October 1, 1973, this had risen to 4,350. This represents a percentage increase of 48.2. Those unaware of the pressure under which we have increased our student intake may wonder why this rate of expansion. It may be illuminating to state here that in 1971 about 11,228 young men and women applied to us for admission. Of these 10,064 were deemed to have met the University's minimum requirements for entry. Yet of this number we could offer admission to only 1,245. This year 17,557 applied to us of which 16,601 possessed the minimum entry requirements. Of the latter number we could offer admission only to 1,431. Thus it has not been easy for us here to find a mean between our sensitivity to the needs of an education-hungry public clamouring for increased intake, and our accountability to the Government and the National Universities Commission which are anxious to match expansion in education with expansion in the national economy.

Nevertheless in spite of our rapid expansion we have not lost sight of national priorities. The ratio of our students in the pure and applied Sciences to those in the Arts and Social Sciences is 59.5: 40.5. The agreed national ratio is 60: 40. The staff-student ratio in this University is 1: 8. The agreed national ratio is 1: 8. In the same manner because we are fully aware of the nation's crying need for qualified teachers of the young, we have as a matter of policy increased our intake of students into the Faculty of Education. In 1971/72 we increased the intake by 22.8%, the following year by 12%.

The increased intake of students made necessary by the need to meet national objectives has necessarily created serious problems for us, especially with regard to hostel accommodation, laboratory, class room and library space and facilities. We are confident that the Government and the philanthropic organisations will come to our aid with even more generous grants and gifts so that we can do the best possible to assuage the thirst of our people for more education and to meet the needs of the nation for highly trained manpower.

Understandably, increase in student numbers has meant that we have had to recruit more staff and even to design programmes for rapid staff training and development. In 1967 the University of Nigeria had about 400 senior staff in its employ of which 75% were Nigerian and 25% expatriate. When the civil war ended in 1970 only 60% of these, that is 240, and all of them Nigerians, reported for duty. To ensure that the staff are able to cope with the increased demands made on them by expansion, we have had to pursue a dynamic staff recruitment policy. Also to ensure that our senior staff establishment enjoys the international character it requires for an active and fruitful existence, we have sought to encourage qualified non-Nigerians to take senior appointments here. As a result by 1971/72 our senior staff strength stood at 455 of which 419 were Nigerian and 36 expatriate - that gave a percentage of 6.78 for expatriates.

By June 30, 1973, our senior staff strength stood at 565 of which 63 were expatriates and 502 Nigerian: that is a percentage of 11.15% for expatriate. Today the senior staff strength is 600 with the percentage of non-indigenous senior staff standing at 12.5%. On the whole since 1970 the University has experienced a senior staff percentage increase of 109.3. Our staff recruitment policy has been based on demonstrable merit and this has borne rich dividends.

We have not only sought to ensure that our staff establishment grew in strength, but also grew in quality. To enable many of the Nigerian staff to rub off rust accumulated during the three years of academic inactivity (1967-1970), we have arranged for them to visit universities and other institutions of higher learning abroad. There, they have had the opportunity to discuss with their colleagues the latest developments in their fields, read new publications and up-date themselves. About 108 of our staff in this category have benefitted from the scheme.

Also we have evolved and launched programmes for training our own staff. It is a well-known fact that Universities and nations, if they can help it do not release their best brains to rivals. We also want to be in a position to have the first choice in training and retraining our best products. To this end, and with the generous cooperation of the National Universities Commission, we worked out the Junior Fellowship Scheme. Under this scheme the ablest graduates in any one year are enabled to return to us for one year during which period they carry minor academic functions under supervision in their respective departments. At the end of the one year, if they prove worthy of further training, they are sent abroad for higher degrees. Since the commencement of the programme 87 Junior Fellows have been appointed. Under the contract guiding the scheme, they are obligated to make the first offer of their services to this University on their return. In addition we have now completed arrangements for running our own full-scale postgraduate programme so that we can supervise the training of our young men and women in order to ensure that their research takes into account national priorities as well as our cultural and social circumstances.

An aspect of the life of our staff which often escapes the notice of our critics is that their energies are not devoted entirely to teaching and research within the so-called ivory walls of the university. In addition to performing this very vital duty, they have remained ever responsive to the calls of patriotic service. Thus my staff continue to render loyal and devoted service to national and state institutions and statutory corporations. Similarly the University has never hesitated to release, for a stated term of years, those staff required by the various governments for full-time service.

HIGHLIGHTS OF ACADEMIC ACHIEVEMENTS

The effort and resources we have so far expended on physical and numerical growth, are already being justified by the academic rewards. Since the end of the civil war, we have graduated, on the average, 728 young men and women yearly. And it is a matter for joy, that many of these secured high grades in spite of the fact that they have had to work under difficult conditions, and had to undergo examinations set, marked and moderated on standards acceptable internationally. The highlights of these results include the following:

in 1970/71 there were 4 in First Class and 99 in Second Class (Upper Division)

in 1971/72 there were 9 in First Class and 90 in Second Class (Upper Division)

in 1972/73 there were 16 in First Class and 130 in Second Class (Upper Division).

Also worthy of mention is the fact that in the Second Professional Examinations for the degrees of Bachelor of Medicine and Bachelor of Surgery for 1971/72, three candidates achieved distinctions in Physiology, and four in Biochemistry - making a total of seven. Of these a female student gained distinction in both Physiology and Biochemistry. In the 1972/73 Second Professional Examinations there were five distinctions in Anatomy, seven in Physiology and twelve in Biochemistry - making a total of twenty-four distinctions. This is the highest number of distinctions in the Second Professional Examination for the degrees of Bachelor of Medicine and Bachelor of Surgery ever recorded in any Nigerian or Commonwealth University with the possible exception of the University of London, as far as I know. It is a record any University can justly be proud of and which no University in Africa North or South of the Sahara is likely to surpass. What was even more remarkable in these results was the fact that a female student Miss Eugenia Onumah scored a distinction in each of the three subjects of Anatomy, Physiology and Biochemistry for which she was awarded the Winthrop Scholarship for Medicine. In the 1972/73 Third Professional Examination for the degrees of Bachelor of Medicine and Bachelor of Surgery there were four distinctions. Two of these, one in Pharmacology the other in Pathology, were won by the same female student Miss B. C. Mbakwem who the previous year gained two distinctions in the Second Professional Examination. Let me emphasise that in all these examinations, the external examiners were from British Universities and were amongst the most eminent in their own fields.

I must pay special tribute to those of my staff who had taught the students so well, and to the students themselves for their industry and discipline whereby these excellent results were achieved. But I must enjoin them to endeavour always to ensure that their academic achievements are matched by their cultivation of good manners, integrity, honesty and moral rectitude which constitute the main cardinal principle of behaviour this University will accept.

The University of Nigeria, like many other Universities started as a primarily teaching University. But in the past three years we have done a great deal to focus attention also on research. This is because we recognise that good research and good teaching are inseparable and because we appreciate the part which original research has to play in solving the many problems of under-development which afflict us in this country. As part of our policy of emphasizing the need for a university to teach and research, we have given every encouragement to those who have responded to our entreaties in this regard. We have made monetary grants to staff for research and attendance at Conferences as well as promoted those who have done distinguished work. As a result of this policy we are on the threshold of significant developments in the investigation of the history, culture and social problems of this part of Nigeria. Also intensive researches are going on in the area of demography, rural administration and curriculum development. It is a measure of the growing recognition which researches in this University are winning that some of them are beginning to attract substantial grants from abroad. Worthy of mention, for instance, is the grant of N28,000.00 from the Medical Research Council of Great Britain to a member of my staff in Zoology for research an parasitic nematodes of man and animals with particular reference to the hookworm. Another grant of N51,152.00 was made by the International Development Research Centre, Canada, to the Department of Political Science towards a research in Institutional Modernisation. A third grant of $223,847 came from the Population Council of New York for the Demographic Research Centre.

THE FEDERAL TAKE-OVER

And now, I come to what, for us the members of this University, is probably the greatest event of the year. By this I am referring to the generous decision of the Federal Government to take-over full responsibility for running the University of Nigeria. The University, came into being in 1960 as an Institution maintained primarily by the Government of the former Eastern Region of Nigeria though its scope and ambitions were national, or even universal as shown by its motto, staff recruitment policy and Student enrolment. At the end of the civil war it became largely the responsibility of the Governments of the East Central and the South-Eastern States. It was with the encouragement of these two states, helped by a Federal subvention to the tune of 33.5% of its annual budget, that the University was rehabilitated to the level described above.

It would be difficult for us to find words adequate for expressing our deep gratitude to the two State Governments. But to say this is not to hide the fact that try however so hard they might, these two governments were never really able to meet their commitments to us. This explains our great relief in becoming the direct responsibility of the Federal Government. I wish to put it on record that this University remains eternally grateful to the Administrator of the East Central State and the Military Governor of the South-Eastern State for recommending and supporting the take-over, to the Federal Military Government, and in particular to our Commander-in-Chief for the decision to convert this institution into a Federal University. For us supported and bouyed up by the Federal Government, as we now are, the sky is only the limit in our effort to live up to the ideals of our founders, to serve the nation and improve humanity.

CHARGE TO THE GRADUANDS

It remains for me to say a few words to the graduands. Ours has been the job of seeing you through this great institution, of planning your curriculum and teaching it, and of guiding the development of your character. We now have the satisfaction of proclaiming that we have found you worthy both in character and learning to hold the degree of this University. What responsibility remains is now yours. You owe a duty to this University to prove yourselves worthy of the trust we now place on you, to the nation and the society to justify the large sums of money spent in your education. Remember always that in order to live up to the motto of this institution you have to serve the nation patriotically and humanity selflessly.

Finally, I want to request you to continue to show a keen interest in the affairs of the University of Nigeria, especially by participating actively in the Alumni Association. This organisation offers you a great opportunity to participate meaningfully and intimately in making the University of Nigeria a place of learning without compare. On behalf of the University I wish you every success in all your legitimate aspirations and efforts.

Your Excellency the Head of State and Commander-in-Chief, the Honourable, Chief Justice of the Federation, Your Excellencies the Administrator of the East Central State and Military Governors, Your Highnesses, My Lords Spiritual and Temporal, distinguished Guests, Ladies and Gentlemen, I thank you all for listening so attentively. I do hope that your short stay with us will be a happy one.

H. C. Kodilinye, Vice-Chancellor.

Office of the Vice-Chancellor December 15, 1973

AN ADDRESS BY THE VICE-CHANCELLOR, UNIVERSITY OF NIGERIA, PROFESSOR H.C. KODILINYE, AT A SPECIAL CONVOCATION TO CONFER AN HONORARY DEGREE ON MAJOR-GENERAL GAAFAR EL-NIMIERY, PRESIDENT OF THE DEMOCRATIC REPUBLIC OF THE SUDAN, 25TH AUGUST, 1973

Your Excellencies, the Heads of State of the Democratic Republic of the Sudan and the Federal Republic of Nigeria, Military Governors, the Administrator, Honourable Commissioners, the Chancellor and the Pro-Chancellor of the University of Nigeria, Deans of Faculties, Members of Staff and Students, Distinguished Guests, Ladies and Gentlemen,We feel very highly honoured by the visit of Your Excellency, Major-General Gafaar El-Nimiery, President of the Democratic Republic of the Sudan. It is therefore with great pleasure that I, on behalf of our entire staff and students, welcome you to this University.

The Federal Republic of Nigeria and the Democratic Republic of the Sudan, over whose affairs you so ably preside, show some common background and experience, and have an association which is long-standing. Also, the University of Nigeria and the University of Khartoum have some meeting points in their background, their inspiration being drawn from the Western tradition.

The Northern part of the Republic of Nigeria falls within the region described as Bilad al-Sudan, stretching south of the Sahara Desert from the Atlantic to the Red Sea and Ethiopia. This region also embraced Cush, which is now in northern Sudan. Cush, in the valley of the Nile, just across Egypt's southern border, was the vital channel through which Egypt influenced and was influenced by the rest of Africa, including our own part of the continent.

The part of Nigeria that was in the old Sudan did not only come under the same influence as the part of the modern Sudan in the same region, nor did it only interact with it, but the Nigerian Sudan also was influenced by what we might call the Sudanese Sudan. The knowledge of iron-working is held to have spread into sub-Saharan Africa from

Meroe, in part of what became the present-day Sudan. This knowledge is believed to have finally come to north-eastern Nigeria and thence to the area of central Nigeria identified with the Nok finds.

The early agricultural civilization which arose around the head-quarters of the Niger River gradually diffused eastward across the entire breadth of the Sudan to the Nile Valley and spread northward to the edge of the Sahara as far as geographical conditions permitted.

The Berbers, who much later occupied portions of the Sahara, and presumably the Egyptians even earlier, established trade relations across the desert with the Sudan.

As this trade developed, its impact was naturally felt first and strongest by the Negro peoples inhabiting the northern fringes of the Sudan. Not only did they enjoy the consequent economic prosperity and benefit from the new products of Mediterranean origin, but they were also in a position to enrich their culture by borrowing adoptive elements from those with whom they traded. Most of them accepted its associated culture. Darfur and Wadai provinces (part of the Democratic Republic of the Sudan) and Bornu and Hausa provinces (part of the Federal Republic of Nigeria) all came under this influence.

Between the desert and the sea, the old Sudan belt was in much earlier times the richest economically, and provided the easiest route for people travelling across the continent from east to west or vice versa, because water holes were not too far apart and the bush was not too thick. This not only fostered interaction between the peoples of the region but also exposed them together to the influence of outsiders who availed themselves of the route.

In medieval times, however, the picture changed with Nubia becoming Christian. As Nubia lay right across the natural east-west trade route south of the Sahara, West African traders from the Muslim states along the River Niger had, at least until the end of the 14th century, to pass northwards across the desert rather than through Christian Nubia. This alternative route took the traders and travellers through centres of Islamic influence and finally to Cairo. They were thus in closer contact with the mainstream of Islamic culture than would have been the case if the southern route had been open to them. An Islamic culture no less than traditional and Christian cultures constitute the total culture of Nigeria and the Sudan today.

Besides, Nigerians on pilgrimage to Mecca travelled by routes passing through the modern Sudan. Some of the Nigerians now settled in the Sudan were those who set out on pilgrimage, especially in the days when pilgrims had to trek to the Holy Land but could not complete the outward or the homeward journey. Today, about two million Nigerians and Sudanese of Nigerian origin are living in the Republic of Sudan.

It is not generally realised that the first Head of Government of the Sudan, on its attainment of independence in 1956, was a citizen of Nigerian origin, and that Nigerians who have been fully integrated into the Sudanese society are today state ministers, top civil servants and business executives. When political parties were functioning, many Nigerians were parliamentarians, chairmen of council and councillors in the Republic.

In more recent times, the two countries had come under colonial rule for the second half of the 19th century to the second half of the twentieth century, a common colonial master being present in both countries.

The sum total of all this is that today many cultural and ethnic links exist between the Federal Republic of Nigeria and the Democratic Republic of the Sudan. There is a strong bond forged by Islam and the Arabic language. A Sudanese was reported recently to have said that he liked Nigeria because General Gowon was handsome and young. He was, continued the Sudanese, like General Nimiery who was also handsome and young! A more significant similarity, however, is the magnanimity of the two Generals, an attribute which will rebound to their eternal credit.

The thirty traumatic months which this country went through recently in civil strife is now history. Some physical reminders of the episode are still with us in these parts, as Your Excellency may have noted. But thanks to the large and generous mind and practical Christianity of our Head of State, the physical effects and, more importantly, the psychological ones, are fast being obliterated. A new nation is being raised from the ruins of war. In the same way, the magnanimity of Your Excellency has brought to an end the civil strife which has raged in your country for seventeen years, slightly pre-dating its resumption of independence. You have not only brought the strife to an end but have also taken bold steps to re-integrate the southerners into the body politic with a view to forging a new nation. This statesmanlike action, which bids fair to succeed, has implications for the whole of Africa. The Sudan is a meeting point between Asia and Africa, in its ethnic composition. When the result of the efforts of Your Excellency is fully realised, that success will be a pointer to those parts of Africa which have to cope with the problem of, as it were, homogenising their diverse populations.

Coming nearer home still, the University of Nigeria and the University of Khartoum have derived their inspiration from the same source, namely, that part of the Western tradition which has English as its medium of communication.

When the latter University was born in 1951, it was as a university college in a special relationship with the University of London. With its attainment of autonomy in 1956, however, it did not break its links with the intellectual traditions of the West: it rather sustained them by arrangements for the exchange of academic staff and graduates with the University of Reading in England, and with Northwestern University, Evanston, and the University of Columbia in the United States.

The University of Nigeria started life in 1960 in association with the Michigan State University, an institution also belonging to the Western tradition. Besides, the University worked in close co-operation with the British Inter-University Council for Higher Education Overseas, which helped it with the recruitment of staff and with the giving of advice over a wide range of problems. More recently, it has established academic links with some universities in the United Kingdom, such as the Universities of Cambridge, Strathclyde and East Anglia.

With our common Western connections, and in keeping with associations being developed among African states in several other spheres, we look forward to the establishment of academic links between the University of Nigeria and the University of Khartoum in the near future.

May I say, Your Excellency, that nothing has given us greater pleasure than this opportunity of knowing you, the Head of a Republic which has so much in common with our own Republic, a statesman who has done so much to bring peace and unity to your country and, through it, probably to the continent of Africa in which it occupies a most strategic cultural and political position.

It is our hope, and indeed wish, that your brief visit to this country and, in particular, to this University will be worthwhile, and that you will return home with abiding memories of it. We on our part will for ever treasure and cherish the memory.

Major-General Gaafar El-Nimiery passed away in June 2009.

Inna Lillami Wa Inna Ilahir Rajiun

(From God we come, unto him we shall return)

THE RECORD OCTOBER 1973

U.N.N. HONOURS PRESIDENT NIMIERY

The success of African educational institutions in general and the universities in particular should be measured by the relevance of their underlying philosophy, goals and objectives to the societies in which they exist'. The President of the Sudan, Sayed Gaafar El Nimiery was speaking at the special Convocation ceremony arranged for him at the University of Nigeria. President Nimiery was awarded as honorary degree of Doctor of Laws by the University. The Head of State, General Yakubu Gowon was present at the ceremony. Welcoming the visitor the Chancellor of the University, Alhaji Ado Bayero spoke of the educational, cultural, economic and social ties linking Nigeria and the Sudan and hoped that the intimate and cordial relations would continue to grow.

In his address the Vice-Chancellor, Prof. Kodilinye observed that the Republic of the Sudan shared a common background and experience with Nigeria. One such similarity which he described as 'significant' was the magnanimity of their two leaders. Prof Kodilinye praised the bold steps President Nimiery has taken to unite South and North in his country.

Receiving the award President Nimiery said that he would cherish and preserve it as another indication of the happy relations existing between Nigeria and the Sudan. President Nimiery said that African universities should be able to respond to the needs of their people and provide effective solutions to the many problems that plague African societies.

In recognition of Herbert's service, President Nimiery bestowed on him his nation's highest award (see picture), The Order of The Two Niles and the following is Herbert's letter of thanks.

President of the Democratic Republic of Sudan

Considering the great service to the nation and to strengthen the bond of friendship we give to you the

Medal of the Two Niles

We establish this Certificate which translates the Nomination in the Peoples' Palace in Khartoum on the 21st August 1973

His Excellency, 20th December, 1973

Sayed Gaafar Mohammed Nimiery,

President of the Democratic Republic of the Sudan,

Khartoum, Sudan.

Your Excellency,

I can hardly find words to express my sincere gratitude for your overwhelming kindness in decorating me with the Order of the Two Niles, Second Class.

The medals and the certifying document were presented to me on the 15th December, 1973. As this happened to be the day our Commander-in-Chief was pleased to receive the honorary degree of Doctor of Laws of this University, your highly valued award constituted additional evidence of the recognition of the significant role of the University , which I have the honour to lead, in the service of Nigeria and humanity.

In all humility, Your Excellency, I feel rather undeserving of your magnanimity. Nevertheless, I can only promise you that my family and I will ever cherish the award, with affection for you and all your peoples.

With my very best wishes,

I remain,

Yours sincerely,

HC Kodilinye

Vice-Chancellor.

Chapter 16

AN ADDRESS BY HIS HIGHNESS ALHAJI ADO BAYERO, C.F.R.. HON. LL.D. (NIGERIA), EMIR OF KANO, CHANCELLOR OF THE UNIVERSITY OF NIGERIA ON THE CCCASION OF THE SPECIAL CONVOCATION FOR THE CONFERMENT OF HONORARY DEGREE ON HIS EXCELLENCY, SAYED GAAFAR MOHAMMED' NIMIERY PRESIDENT OF THE DEMOCRATIC REPUBLIC OF THE SUDAN ON SATURDAY 25TH AUGUST, 1973

Your Excellencies, Honourable Visitors to the University, My Lords Spiritual and Temporal, Distinguished Guests, Ladies and Gentlemen.

Today, 25th August, 1973, will go down in the history of this University as one of those days ever to be remembered. It is a great honour for us in this University to receive, at this Special Convocation, our distinguished guests, His Excellency, Sayed Gaafar Mohammed Nimiery, President of the Democratic Republic of the Sudan and Madam Busaina Khalid Nimiery. We are also equally extremely delighted to welcome our Head of State, His Excellency, General Yakubu Gowon and Mrs, Gowon, and we take this opportunity to observe that this is the first visit of His Excellency, General Yakubu Gowon, to this University since the Federal Military Government took over the management of the University.

Relations between Nigeria and the Sudan have been long and varied*
Trade along well-worn caravan routes linked the two countries centuries
ago and pious pilgrims made their way to the Holy Land through the
Sudan. Very little, however, is known of these contacts before the
sixteenth century when the Islamic Sultanate of Darfur established itself.
During this period, it is believed that regular trade existed between the
Sudan and the Kingdom of Bornu, but the details of these transactions
seem to be buried in obscurity.

In the religious and academic fields, our relations with the Sudan
have been very intimate and cordial. It is an established fact that
pilgrims from Nigeria passed through the Sudan on their journey to
Mecca and Medina. Many of those who chose to go via Egypt did so
after touching on Sudan territory around El-Obeid and Shendi, The
existence of many Nigerians in the Sudan today is due mainly to the
fact that Sudan is on the major pilgrim route taken by Nigerians, mainly
Hausa and Fulani from the Northern States. Some of them, who were
unable to reach Mecca, settled in the Sudan. Others settled in the Sudan
after performing their pilgrimage, apparently attracted by the famous
hospitality of the Sudanese.

Intercourse between Nigeria and the Sudan gained in tempo from
the beginning of the twentieth century when, in addition to the reasons
of pilgrimage and trade, another motive emerged, that of migrations in
flight from the British invaders. One good example was that of Sultan
Attahiru I of Sokoto, who set out to emigrate to Mecca rather than accept
subjugation by the British. He was joined by thousands of Nigerians
from Katsina, Kano, Bauchi and other cities in the Northern States
who were opposed to British rule. Although the Sultan and some of his
followers were eventually killed by the British, the survivors persevered
to Sudan. On arriving there, they went to the region of Sennar where they
founded a town. They gave it the name Mai Wurno which was borrowed
from Wurno of Sokoto-, the town of Muhammed Bello, the Sultan.
Mai-Wurno still exists in the Sudan and the Sudanese pronounce it as
Mayirno. It is still inhabited by Nigerians, mostly Hausa and Fulani. A
visit to this town will find the people speaking not Arabic, but Hausa

and Fulani* In recent years, Sudanese Arabs have also settled in the town. In Mayirno, a sultanate has been established and recognized by the Sudanese Government. The last Sultan Tahir, descendant of Tahir I, died only recently. In addition to Mayirno, one finds communities of Nigerian origin in the regions of Kasala Hasahisa, Kasala, Duwaym and several Others. These communities greatly help in the agricultural development of the country.

On the educational side, our relations with the Sudan have been happier still. Educational relations must have existed side by side with trade and religious contacts, but it was distinctly marked in 1934, when at the instance of my father, the Emir of Kano, Abdullah Bayero, and the Emir of Katsina, Muhammed Dikko, three Sudanese Sheikhs were allowed by the Sudanese Government to come and serve in Nigeria. Their mission was to establish a law school on the pattern then used in the Sudan. Katsina was considered a suitable location for the School, when the three Sheikhs, Sheikh Bashir El-Rayyah, Sheikh Muhammed Siwar al-dhahab and Sheikh al-Nur al-Tingari, arrived at Kano, they stayed for three nights with my father and then continued to Katsina. Later, they returned to Kano and established the Law School there. They were followed by two other Sheikhs, Sheikh Awad Muhammad Ahmed and Sheikh Abdulhamid. These two died after returning to their country – may their souls rest in peace. The School, which they established, continued to provide the Northern States with Alkalis and teachers. It is this law school which developed into the School for Arabic Studies. Later, part of it became Ahmadu Bello College and is now the Abdullahi Bayero College, named after my father in recognition of his great role in the founding of the College from which all these developments stemmed, Sudanese scholars are still among the members of the teaching staff in both the School for Arabic Studies and the Abdullahi Bayero College.

It is worthy of note that when the Abdullahi Bayero College was established as a College of Ahmadu Bello University, it was a great Sudanese scholar in the person of Professor Abdulla El-Tayib who came to be its first Provost. He saw the College through the first two years of its development as part of the University, In this effort, in addition to

Nigerians and other nationals, Professor El-Tayib was assisted by four other Sudanese. Thus, it is not only in the field of Arabic and Islamic Studies that Sudanese scholars have contributed to the educational development of this.country; they are also to be found in the Universities, the Secondary Schools, and the Ministries, teaching or serving in the fields of engineering, law, agriculture, veterinary science, medicine and health. Our debt to the Sudanese Government in the supply of personnel cannot be over-estimated, and. it is to be said to their credit that they always send us their best men. Professor El-Tayib is unique in his field and yet the Government made him available to us for two years. When the then North Regional Government requested the Sudan to provide a person to serve on the panel for the revision of our penal code, it was their Chief who was sent.

Your Excellency, it is not only in the supply of personnel that we are indebted to your country but also in the training of our own people in your own country. In 1954, six of our students went to Bakhter Ruda Institute of Education and joined Kulli-yat at Sanatayn. They all came back with diplomas and tney are now people we are proud of in this country. This process continued and and several other Nigerians have studied in your country and returned with their diplomas. In subsequent years, Nigerian students started going to the University of Khartoum to read for their first, and, in some cases, their second degrees. This practice still continues, and only three weeks ago, a batch of five undergraduates from Ahmadu Bello College left for the Sudan to spend six months in the University of Khartoum to improve their proficiency in Arabic language and literature.

Our cordial relations in all fields have come to stay and we hope that the process will continue to grow into a two-way channel. This is surely happening. There are several Sudanese students studying in Abdullahi Bayero College. One of them has already graduated and is now an Assistant Lecturer in the same College. In the commercial fields, we are happy to see that a large number of Sudanese businessmen are in our midst. It pleases us most to see that some of them have become very successful and they own several companies and enterprises. Our hope is that the cordial relations will continue to grow from strength to strength.

Your Excellencies, Honourable Visitors to the University, My Lords Spiritual and Temporal, Distinguished Guests, Ladies and Gentlemen, I feel that I should not conclude my address without revealing the fact that I, myself, am a graduate of the School for Arabic Studies. Consequently, I find it most appropriate to conclude in Arabic.

وَأَخِيرًا سِيَادَةَ الرَّئِيـــسِ

إِنَّ أَيَادِيكُمْ عِنْدَنَا لَكَثِيرَةٌ جِدًّا

وَلَا نَمْلِكُ إِلَّا التَّعْبِيرَ عَنْ شُكْرِنَا الْعَمِيقْ

لِسِيَادَتِكُمْ وَلِلشَّعْبِ السُّودَانِي السَّقِيقْ ،

وَلَكِنَّ الْكَلِمَاتِ قَاصِرَةٌ عَنِ الْإِفْصَاحِ عَمَّا فِي

صُدُورِنَا 🐉 مِنَ التَّقْدِيرِ وَالشُّكْرِ لَكُمْ .

وَلَا يَسَعُنَا إِلَّا أَنْ نَسْأَلَ اللَّهَ تَبَارَكَ وَتَعَالَى

أَنْ يَجْعَلَ بِلَادَنَا وَبِلَادَكُمْ فِي أَمْنٍ دَائِمٍ وَرَغْدِ

عَيْشٍ مُسْتَمِرْ . وَيُدِيمَ كَنَدَكَ عَلَى قَتَنَا الطَّيِّبَةَ

إِلَى الْأَبَدْ . وَالسَّلَامُ عَلَيْكُمْ وَرَحْمَةُ اللَّهِ وَبَرَكَاتُهُ ،

UNIVERSITY OF NIGERIA

AN ADDRESS BY THE VICE-CHANCELLOR, PROFESSOR H.C. KODILINYE, GIVEN AT THE UNIVERSITY OF NIGERIA, NSUKKA ON CONVOCATION DAY, 14 DECEMBER, 1974

Your Excellencies, Your Highness, the Emir of Kano and Chancellor of the University, Chairman of the Provisional Council, my Lords Spiritual and Temporal, Distinguished Guests, Members of the University, Ladies and Gentlemen:

May I say how pleased I am to welcome you all to this Convocation for the conferment of degrees, the tenth in the annals of this University. We are gratified that so many distinguished men and women are able to honour our invitation and grace this occasion with their presence. We always look forward to the opportunity of sharing your company at our Convocation which has become one of the most important events in our calendar.

During the 1973 Convocation when this University had the satisfaction of conferring degrees honoris causa on two of this country's most distinguished citizens – His Excellency General Yakubu Gowon, Head of the Federal Military Government and Commander-in-Chief of the Armed Forces and the Honourable the Chief Justice of the Federation – I reported that we had in most cases attained the pre-civil war condition in our physical state while in a few areas we had even surpassed that. To illustrate this, I went through the physical and academic reconstruction we had successfully undertaken as well as our achievements academically in staff development. I also reported what one regarded as a great event in our history – the assumption by the Federal Military Government of full responsibility for running the University. With this takeover, financial support for the institution has become assured and we are now poised to take off into sustained development.

DEVELOPMENT OF THE UNIVERSITY

PHYSICAL GROWTH

The development of our physical structures to provide necessary facilities for meaningful functioning of the University continued unabated. Our fledgling Department of Pharmacy needed adequate facilities to win the approval of the Pharmacists Board of Nigeria for the training of graduate Pharmacists. We undertook the provision of these facilities which included the putting up of eight blocks of buildings and equipping laboratories in them. These facilities were inspected by the Pharmacists Board early last May and approved. Another area in which the University needed adequate facilities to turn out professionals badly needed by the country, is in the Veterinary Sciences. A Veterinary Teaching Hospital and teaching/laboratory and offices for the three departments in these sciences are about to be completed and equipped ready for inspection by the Veterinary Council of Nigeria as an establishment for the training of Veterinary Surgeons registrable with the Council. The main Faculty of Agricultural Sciences (Cardoso) Building which was considerably damaged by: fire has almost been completely reconstructed.

Other construction works undertaken during the year included an animal house for the Department of Biochemistry, Microbiology and Pharmacy, which has been completed, and additional classrooms for the Faculty of Agricultural Sciences and teaching/laboratory and offices for each of the Departments of Animal Science, Crop Science and Soil Science, which are nearing completion. A Department of Geology building is about to be completed, and Physics Observatory and Transmitting Hut and Greenhouse for the Department of Botany are at advanced stage. A Medical Library at Enugu is in hand and Physics laboratory and offices, a building for the Department of Languages and Office for the Dean of Arts and a Department of Music building are about to be started.

Since my last address, 37 staff housing units which were at their initial stages at that time had been completed and about 30 others are nearing completion, bringing the total since to 67 and the total since

April 1971 to 135. In spite of all these, however, we are not yet out of the woods in this respect.

Hostels for students are as much the responsibility of the University as quarters for staff. To meet this responsibility, 20 blocks of flats at Nsukka often spoken of as Onuiyi Haven complexes have been taken over temporarily by the University and repaired to provide accommodation for 800 students. A new hostel block was started at the Enugu Campus about the middle of the year and will be ready for occupation in February. The construction of two more hostels at Enugu and two at Nsukka will commence soon.

But our effort to meet our immediate needs will in no way deter us from the major physical development of the campus which I mentioned during my last address. We are committed to restructuring the University in a way that aims aesthetically at elegance and majesty and functionally at improved quality of teaching and better staff/student understanding. The first phase of this development programme, which fits into the Third National Development Plan, and which has been approved by the Provisional Council, provides for the following:

The first four colleges;

The Science Building;

Shopping Centre, and

The Auditorium.

It is the intention that the execution of this phase will start during this session. Our programme is not calculated to change adversely the intrinsic character of the University: it rather would enhance it. We do not intend to rub off those venerable rusts that preserve rather than destroy the metal.

With all humility I must sincerely thank all those whose encouragement, steadfastness and faith in the future and destiny of this great institution has sustained us and strengthened our resolve during these gruelling years in our determined effort to plan for an institution which will structurally and philosophically stand out in eminence and constitute the pride of a great country yearning for true education and enlightenment for the citizens of this generation and the generation to come. For my part I am eternally grateful for the Federal Military Government for its magnanimity and for the confidence it reposed on us by giving us the chance and opportunity to re-establish ourselves and rehabilitate this institution, the portals of which are wide open to all Nigerians.

Our laboratories continue to acquire more equipment and the Library has added to its stock of 40,577 volumes as at my last address, 11,728 volumes, 90% of which are books and the rest bound journals. Recognising the need for a computer in a technological and jet age, the University opened a Computer Centre last September. The Computer was installed on arrangement with the IBM.

We have not confined our physical development to the erection of new structures and equipping them. We have also aimed at providing other amenities that will facilitate the functioning of the University community. Having regard not only to the good maintenance or its plants and services but more importantly to the health of the members of the community, the University has embarked on a programme ultimately aimed at making it self-sufficient in water supply. To this end, in addition to one borehole commissioned last year, a second borehole is under construction and but for the failure of the contractors it should have been ready for commissioning by now and a third taken in hand. We have invited another company in the field to undertake preliminaries preparatory to their sinking more boreholes for us. If their investigations prove fruitful, they will be commissioned to sink two more boreholes. It is hoped that when the additional boreholes are put into service the water needs of the University for some years to come will be fully met, But to take care of the continued growth of the University until it attains its maximum size, it is our proposal to sink seven boreholes on the whole, progressively as the size of the community may dictate.

The University is mindful of the safety and health of the community in other ways. Because Nsukka lies in a region of intense thunderstorm activity, which makes the probability of loss of life and damage to property by lightning strikes relatively high, the University undertook a scheme of lightning protection which was to be executed in two phases. The first phase which covered a much greater part of the Campus has been completed and the second phase which will take care of the rest is about to be undertaken. Also the lighting of the streets of the campus has for the first time become a reality. The illumination of our streets has given the whole campus a more attractive picture. Conscious of our responsibility for the health and care of the community, we have embarked upon a mass chest X-ray programme covering the entire staff and their families and the students in all the three campuses of the University, the aim being to isolate pulmonary tuberculosis and give it immediate attention to prevent complications and check its spread in the community. Additionally, our Department of Ophthalmology is carrying out glaucoma survey to detect early, for treatment, this dreadful disease which leads inexorably to total blindness if not dealt with in time.

ACADEMIC GROWTH

We have also leapt forward in other areas of physical development. The physical structures and equipment became necessary so that students may be admitted and staff appointed to teach and take care of them in other ways. In other words, what we have provided have the needs of the nation as its end. Because of the unusually large number of qualified applicants seeking admission to University we admitted considerably many more students than we admitted last year. Whereas the total admissions offered last year was 1975 out of a total of about 14,000 qualified applicants, the total admissions offered this year is 2,270 out of a total of over 18,000 applicants deemed to have met the University's minimum entry requirements, a percentage increase of 12.3. It was not easy for us to harmonise our consciousness of the needs of an education-hungry population with the optimum intake which our limited facilities can accommodate.

Our enrolment figure which at the beginning of the 1973/74 session stood at 4,678, 3,894 of whom were men and 784 women, rose to 5,791 (4802 male and 989 female) at the beginning of this session, representing a percentage increase of about 23.6, and nearly doubling the enrolment figure for 1970/71 session (which was 2,934).

With an eye on making our production of high level manpower keep in line with expansion in the national economy our intake of students was weighted in favour of the pure and applied sciences where the total number offered admission for this session is 1,321 against 949 in the arts and the social sciences. This gives a ratio of 58;42, quite near to the agreed national ratio of 60:40. The University being an instrument for national development is certainly sensitive to national priorities.

It is our hope that the nation will appreciate the problems the rapid increase if the intake of students pose for the University and will give it its sympathy and understanding in its effort to grapple with these problems. The University no doubt will gird its loins and bend its sinews to meet fully the obligations which increased student numbers place upon it.

The extent of our manpower output in some measure reflects our academic growth. The University graduated 740 students in June 1973 and is graduating 774 today. Of the latter, seven men and one woman made a First Class Honours while 112 men and 40 women made a Second Class Honours (Upper Division) Degrees.

In the Second Professional examination in Medicine taken last April, 22 distinctions – 5 in Anatomy, 7 in Physiology and 10 in Biochemistry – were achieved in a class of 107 of which 96 passed and 11 were referred with no failures. Of those who made distinctions, Messrs B.E.A. Emeasoba and E.O. Ozo achieved that in all three subjects. In the examination for the degree of Doctor of Veterinary Medicine held last June, four of the 10 successful candidates at the Part Two of the examination were awarded five distinctions, four in Animal Production and one in Animal Nutrition. In the Part Three of the same examination, three out of the six successful candidates achieved 10 distinctions, three in Veterinary Bacteriology, three in Veterinary Virology, two in Veterinary Toxicology, one in Veterinary Pathology and one in Veterinary Pharmacy. One student, John Osita Okoye, achieved five distinctions. An external examiner wrote about the latter examination:

"The better students were most impressive and J.N.O. Okoye would still have achieved the best result had he presented himself for examination with my students in Dublin. At the request of the Nsukka staff, I examined at the level applied in Dublin and Glasgow and would conclude this section by complimenting the students in having attained a standard which matches ours while under far less satisfactory conditions."

At the end of the last calendar year our senior staff strength stood at 600 about 450 of whom were teaching staff. Today the number is 729, 569 of whom are teaching staff, giving a percentage rise of 21.5 on the total senior staff strength and of 26.4 on the teaching staff strength. This means that our teaching staff student ratio this year has improved over last year's. Our present total staff strength of 729 is approaching double the strength of 400 in 1967.

In an effort to recruit enough teaching staff to cover as adequately as possible all the courses for the students to be enrolled for 1974/75, the University carried out a rigorous recruitment drive which resulted in a large number of appointments. Some of those appointed have assumed duties. The main obstacle in the way of the expatriate appointees joining us is the long time it takes for them to obtain entry permits/visa into the country. Understandably, the Federal Government is careful about the security of the State and the processes adopted to safeguard this are necessarily slow. Nevertheless, it is our hope that before too long more of the appointees will be able to come into the country and help to alleviate our problem in this regard.

While we appoint new staff we lose some old ones through resignation. This, within limits, is not at all a disturbing phenomenon in a University. Academics anywhere are generally migratory animals and, in some sense, this is good for the Universities and the academics themselves. A few illustrations may both bear out the migratory tendency of academics as well as indicate that the percentage turnover for this University is not alarming compared with that of some other Universities. In 1972 this University lost 11 teaching staff against a' teaching staff strength of about 420. At the end of the last session, against a teaching staff strength of about 500, the University lost about 30 staff by resignation. In 1972, the most recent year for which figures are available to me. University of Ife lost 64 out of a strength of 305, Ahmadu Belio University 28 out of a strength of 540, University of Ghana 32 out of 456, University of Cambridge 48 out of approximately 1200 and University of Zambia 43 out of 200.

STAFF DEVELOPMENT AND TRAINING

As I said during my address in 1972, it was clear to. me quite early on my assumption of office that the good name of the University would depend, to a considerable extent, on the quality of its staff. Consequently, staff training and development became the conncrstone of our policy. This stance motivated the Junior Fellowship Scheme which we worked out and which I had already spoken about on previous occasions of this type.

Last year, I reported that 87 Junior Fellows had been appointed since the commencement of the programme. Since then additional 26 have been appointed. Of all these a total number of 71 are now undertaking postgraduate studies in various Universities largely in the Western World. As our postgraduate programme expands, we shall be able increasingly to undertake the training of these Junior Fellows here, although we shall still find it necessary to send some of them to other Universities to diversify the training and background available to the University in its teaching staff.

The University has also had the postgraduate training of her staff sponsored by various other bodies, for which she is grateful. Some of such bodies are the Federal Government, the German Academic Exchange Service (DAAD), the Canadian International Development Agency (CIDA) the Royal Netherlands Government, the Inter-University Council and the British Council.

Apart from our academic staff who are undertaking postgraduate training leading to higher degrees, there are others on study leave to enable them to exchange ideas with colleagues in other Universities and update their competence in their own field thereby becoming more effective in their service to the University. Members of our senior administrative, technical and library staff have also had opportunities to up-date their knowledge and practice in other Universities, during study leave supported by the University.

We have not limited our staff development and training to the senior staff. The Intermediate and Junior Staff have their own opportunities. During the year, 58 Intermediate and Junior Staff were given study leave with pay to enable them to undertake various studies, largely overseas but also in the country; while 11 others are on in-service training.

UNIVERSITY AS AN INTERNATIONAL COMMUNITY

There has been considerable heat engendered recently in some quarters through misinformation about our recruitment policy. True to the provisions of our Law, no discrimination is and shall be allowed either in staff appointment or in student admission, on racial, ethnic, religious or political grounds. Although our appointments have been guided by this principle, it is interesting to note that in the session 1971/72, out of a senior staff Strength of 455, 419 were Nigerian and 36 expatriate, making expatriates 6.78% of the total strength. At the end of 1973 expatriates made up 75 of a total senior Staff strength of 600, giving them a percentage of 12.5. Today, 94 of them form about 12.8% of a total senior staff strength *of* 729. In 1967, out of about 400 senior staff in the University's employ, 75% were Nigerian and 25% expatriate.

Out of a total of 11 Deans, 10 are Nigerian; all four Directors of Institutes and Division in the University are Nigerian, and out of a total of 59 Heads of Departments, 10 are expatriate while 49 are Nigerian, We shall continue to appoint our staff on merit. To do otherwise will be most disasterous and a betrayal of the trust placed in us by the nation to provide the best possible tertiary education for this generation and the generation to come. As Disraeli put it, a University should be a place of light, of liberty and of learning. I should enlarge on this and say that a University should be a place devoid of bigotry and prejudice.

BENEFACTIONS

This University continues to benefit from the goodwill of friends at home and abroad. I do not have enough time to list all these benefactions which we have already appropriately acknowledged, but it seems necessary to mention a few.

1. The British Government: Polarising microscopes complete with electronic attachments, valued at 7,000.00, for the use of our Department of Geology.

2. UNICEF: One Landrover and a Voiture Peugeot for the supervision of the Young Farmer's Club and Home and Food Sciences Extension Programme in Okpuje Demonstration Area.

3. The British Council: A large assortment of expensive sports equipment for cricket and lawn tennis.

4. South-Eastern State Government: A motor vehicle for the use of Diploma students in Animal Health and Husbandry on practical assignment.

5. German academic Exchange Service (DAAD): Educational equipment work DM 12,399.50.

6. United bank for Africa Ltd. 10,000.00 per annum for the payment of the salary of a Lecturer in Banking to be appointed by the University.

7. His Excellency, Sayed Gaafar Mohamed Nimeri: Books worth 2,500.00.

I had on previous occasions mentioned several bilateral technical aid agreement which this University had entered into through the Federal Military Government. I did not then include the agreement with the Government of Japan By this agreement, this University co-operates with the Government of Japan in the field of basic medical education. The co-operation will last for a period of five years beginning from

December 1972. The Government of Japan will send two or three experts annually in the field of basic medical sciences from 1973 and will supply annually, equipment for basic medical education. Training facilities will also be provided in Japan for up to 10 Nigerian doctors and technicians from this University in the field of basic medical science during the period of co-operation.

We are most grateful to the donors for their generous benefactions. OBITUARY:

I regret to report the loss by death of 13 members of the University during the year under review. These are made up of two professors, Professor S. Orajaka of our Department of Geology and Professor Thirion de Briel of our Department of Languages; four students, namely, Mr. Eze Obiora of the Faculty of Law, Mr. Victor Unigwe, postgraduate student in Political Science, Mr. Cornelius N. Onwuka of the Department of Plant/Soil Science and Mr. Chukwuma Ogugua of the Department of Mechanical Engineering, and seven Intermediate and Junior staff Mr, Patrick Odo, Miss Bernedette N. Okorafor, Mr. Daniel Ezeikpe, Mr* John Ugwu, Mr. Emmanuel Alumona, Mr. Ake A.K., and Mr. Kalu Okercke Kalu.

May their souls rest in peace.

CHARGE TO THE GRADUANDS:

I should not come to the end of this address without saying a word or two to you, the graduands. I should begin with congratulating you on the successful completion of your courses and the prize winners on the extra achievement.

You are leaving the confines of this University for the wider world and for your success in your journey through it you have the best wishes of this University. The strength of your education and training will be tested when you come to grips with stark realities of life. It is our hope that you will fight the good fight with all your might and in your success in various facets of life bear laudable testimony to this institution.

It has been our pleasant duty to supervise the development of your mind and the moulding of your character. We are now about to proclaim you worthy both in character and learning to hold the degree of this University. It should be your resolve that our labours should not be in vain. You can cover your alma mater with glory or with shame depending on'how you play your part in the larger society into which you are about to step. If while you strive to make your material mark in life you lay at least equal stress on service to humanity, you will both realize yourself and uplift this institution, I have no doubt that you will succeed once the resolution is there. Go you therefore into the world, serve and prosper.

Finally, I hope that in leaving the University you will not be turning your back on it. You should not only follow its progress with interest but should do so.

Your Excellencies, Your Highness, the Emir of Kano and Chancellor of the University, the Chairman of the Provisional Council, my Lords Spiritual and Temporal, Distinguished Guests, Members of the University, Ladies and Gentlemen, once more, it is our pleasure having you in our midst. Thank you all for listening so patiently.

H. C. Kodilinye, Vice Chancellor.

OFFICE OF THE VICE-CHANCELLOR

14 DECEMBER, 1974.

HONORARY DEGREES

HONORARY DEGREES CONFERRED BY UNIVERSITY OF NIGERIA 1971-1973 DURING THE VICE-CHANCELLORSHIP OF PROFESSOR H.C. Kodilinye

Major General Yakubu Gowon, Head of State, Commander in Chief of the Armed Forces. Chairman of African Unity – Hon (LL.D) 1973

The Military Governor of the South East State, Brigadier U.J. Esuene – Hon (LL.D) 1971

The Mid-Western Governor Colonel U.Obemudia – Hon (LL.D) 1971

The Administrator of the East-Central State Mr Ukpabi Asika – Hon (D.Lit) 1971

The Vice-Chancellor Ahmadu Bello University Prof. Audu – Hon (D.Sc) 1971

The Vice-Chancellor University of Ife Prof. Oluasami – Hon (D.SC) 1971

Major-General Gaafar El-Nimiery, President of the Democratic Republic of the Sudan 1973

Sir Louis Mbanefo – Hon (LL.D)

Dr Elias, Chief Justice of the Federation Hon (D.Lit.)

Chapter 17

The Teaching Hospital, Enugu

PHYSICAL GROWTH

As the University of Nigeria , before the civil war, did not have a Faculty of Medicine it was decided that this was to be a major part of the physical growth of the University. Owing to severe financial and other constraints it was not possible to undertake the building of a Teaching Hospital in the immediate future. Hence the Government of the East Central State agreed that the Enugu Specialist Hospital be made available for a period of five years and it commenced as such under a Board of Governors constituted by the University Governing Council. This arrangement was the best way to ensure the adequate facilities and expertise, which only the University could provide, were available for the training of young men and women to become not only competent doctors but also good citizens. Because medical Science was so complex the control of the Teaching Hospitals at that time passed to the Universities.

Since the inception of the Medical Faculty in 1970/71 the yearly intake of students averaged 700. Many of these secured high grades in spite of the difficult conditions.

In 1970/71   4   students gained First Class

99 students gained Second Class (upper)

In 1971/72   9   students gained First Class

90 students gained Second Class (upper)

In 1972/73   16 students gained First Class

130 students gained Second Class (upper).

3 candidates gained distinction in Physiology, and 4 in Biochemistry. Of these a femal student gained distinctionboth in Physiology and Biochemistry.

In 1972/73 there were 5 distinctions in Anatomy, ten in Physiology and 12 in Biochemistry.

This is the highest number of distinctions in the Second Professional exam for the degree of Batchelor of Medicine and Batchelor of Surgery ever recorded in any Nigerian or Commonwealth University at that time with the exception of the University of London.

In 1975 the University of Nigeria Teaching Hospital graduated its first class of nurses. The presentation of Certificates, Badges and Medals was performed by Her Excellency Mrs Victoria Gowon on Saturday 5th April 1975.

The progress owes much to the dedication of those whose task it was to see the hospital through its early difficult period. It is also due to the judicious management of resources as well as the support of the Federal and East Central State Governments and organizations such as UNICEF.

The University completed the necessary arrangements to conduct its first degree examination in June 1975. About 50 pioneer students were involved in the exercise. The external examiners were from Britain:-

Professor Ruth Bowden and Professor D.N.Baron of the Royal Free Hospital Medical School, London University and Dr.B.Mackenna of the Institute of Physiology, Glasgow University.

The Teaching Hospital by 1975 was a 500-bed hospital. The new buildings included an ultra-modern operating theatre complex. It was here that the first open-heart surgery in tropical Africa was performrd in February 1974.

As the only hospital of its kind in the Eastern States, its task was great. The figures of 12,626 in-patients and 153,137 out-patients for 1976 attested to that.

General Gowon visits Britain

H.M. Queen Elizabeth gave a state banquet at Buckingham Palace in honour of the Head of the Federal Military Government, Commander-in-Chief of the Armed Foces of the Federal Republic of Nigeria and Mrs Gowon.

His Excellency, General Yakubu Gowon Head of the Federal Military Government and Commander-in-Chief of the Armed Forces of the Federal Republic of Nigeria

Prof. H. C. Kodilinye Vice-Chancellor University of Nigeria 1970

His Excellency, Sayed Gaafar Mohammed Nimiery President of the Democratic Republic of Sudan

H. C. Kodilinye, M.B., Ch.B., D.O. (Oxon.), D.O.M.S. (England) Vice-Chancellor, University of Nigeria

Chief N. U. Akpan, O.F.R., B.A.,
B.Sc. (Lond.) Pro-Chancellor,
University of Nigeria

Church service (St. Peter's) at U.N.N. 1973
The Vice Chancellor and his wife

A.G.R.D Kodilinye senior lecturer Faculty of Law U.N.N. attending
The Convocation Ceremony

The Univerity of Nigeria Police Band

Hon. Graduates of U.N.N.

1973 at U.N.N. Convocation
Gen Gowon the U.N.N. (visitor) Chief Ukpabi Asika (administrator E.C.S)
Chief Justice Elias later Chief Justice at The Hague

Mrs R Kodilinye being presented to U.N.N. Soccer Team before taking
the 'Kick off' June 1972

Gen Yakubu Gowon Head of State & Commander in Chief of the Armed Forces receives the Hon. Degree (L.L.D) U.N.N. presented by Alhaji Ado Bayero Emir of Kano, Chancellor University of Nigeria

Dr Elies being conferred with Hon Degree at U.N.N.

Sir Louis Mbanefo Hon. (LL.D) U.N.N.

Graduation luncheon Ninth Convocation U.N.N. 16.xii.73 held in the Niger Room

St Peters inside the University Chapel

U.N.N. Special Convocation 25.viii.73
Their Excellencies – Sayed Gaffar Nimiery, Gen Gowan and
Ukpabi Asika

Elaine attending Convocation

The Vice Chancellor U.N.N. giving his addres at Convocation 1973

3 Graduates U.N.N. at the Convocation Ceremony

At Lagos, Award Ceremony Vice Chancellor H.C.K.

Chapter 18

The Red Cross

It was not long after Herbert took over the Vice-Chancellorship of the University and staff and students were settled in that Justice Akbakoba, a High Court Judge and Chairman of the Red Cross (Croix Rouge) for the Federation of Nigeria with a population of 137 million, asked me if I would take over the Chairmanship of the Nsukka Division of the Red Cross which I thought was a gigantic task. I was overwhelmed by this request and wished to ponder over the possibility of being able to accept.

As the wife of the Head of the University, I was already appointed the Patron of the University Women's Association, which held regular meetings to discuss and solve problems which presented themselves from time to time. I was expected to address opening ceremonies, exhibitions and various other functions and to visit the sick when necessary but I must not forget the invitations to take the 'Kick Off' at many inter-university football matches. I realised that this would consume most of my time and, therefore, it would not be possible to accept Justice Akbakoba's offer.

I was a member of the Red Cross in England and performed my duty during the second World War but that was a different situation from that which I would meet in Nigeria. The Red Cross was born on

24 June 1859 in Switzerland and the Nigerian Red Cross Society with its headquarters in Lagos was founded in 1960 and was recognised internationally. The Red Cross is an international Organisation for the treatment of the sick and wounded in war and for helping those affected by large-scale national disasters.

At that time in Nigeria just after Independence in 1960 there was a shortage of doctors in the outlying districts of the towns and because of this there were many deaths of mothers after childbirth. As a consequence, much of the work of the Red Cross in the Federation was to care for these motherless babies. In the east of the country, which was mainly Roman Catholic, efforts were made to build homes for these infants where they would be cared for up to their first year and then would be sent back home to their grandparents to be brought up. I was already looking after the motherless daughter of one of my gardeners, whom I named Rosaline after my mother, who had long since 'passed to glory'

Having always been interested in the welfare of children, I felt I should accept the invitation offered to me by the Chairman of the Federal Red Cross, Justice Akbakoba and I did so. It was gladly welcomed and I set to work. At this point I would like to say, in retrospect, that it was the most gratifying and rewarding effort I have taken on. To save the life of one child now reaching 38 years of age means so much and in my time in office there were many more including triplets and twins.

As a member of the University community I took the liberty of requesting help from them. I needed immediately an office, a workshop and transport. As expected, this was granted and I was most grateful. Finance at this stage was essential too. It occurred to me that I should put in an Appeal to the public in my division for financial aid to build our own Motherless Babies Home for these unfortunate children, using baby Rosaline as an example. Rosaline was accommodated in a state baby home in her infancy. The following is a copy of my Appeal:-

THE NIGERIAN RED CROSS SOCIETY

NSUKKA DIVISION

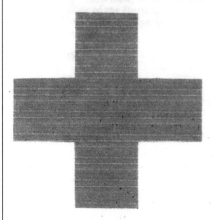

Help to save these Children!

Baby Rosaline

The life of this child was saved by the Nigerian Red Cross. Her mother died and left this unfortunate baby at the tender age of **3 weeks**. When it seemed that there was little or no hope of her survival, a place was found for her in the Motherless Babies' Home in Enugu. Here she was cared for by dedicated and experienced hands and happily we report that she was recently discharged to her home, at the age of **18 months** a strong healthy child. But this is only one case of the hopelessly helpless babies in our community. There are many more daily coming to the notice of the Nigerian Red Cross, Nsukka Division. Out of approximately 30 beds in the Enugu Home which caters for a vast area of the East Central State, how can we expect accommodation for all the motherless babies who are on our books in Nsukka Division alone? We cannot, however, close our eyes to the fact that these babies need our help urgently for they have a right to survival.

How can You help?

We the Nigerian Red Cross Nsukka Division, are launching our 2-year development programme. We propose building a Motherless Babies' Home, a Child Welfare Clinic, Divisional Red Cross Secretariat and Disaster Relief Centre at Nsukka. To this end, and with the kind co-operation of the Government, a plot of land has been allocated to us free. Our Red Cross members are striving by all means possible to raise funds to put up the buildings as quickly as possible. Within the last 10 months we have raised ₦2,000. While this seems a valiant effort, it is only a small portion of the target of ₦30,000 which we have set ourselves initially. We are redoubling our efforts to reach this target but time is against us for we realise that many innocent babies are to die for want of skilled care in a Motherless Babies' Home.

Do Come To Our Aid Quickly In Whatever Way You Can—Money, Building Materials, Free Labour etc. etc.

The Life of someone dear to you may be one of those we can help to save. Please remember that the JOY OF SAVING LIFE is immeasurable.

Donations, both great and small, will be thankfully received. Cheques, Money Orders, Postal Orders should be made payable to: The N. R. C. N. D. A receipt will be issued to all donors and their names published. Please send your donations to:

Mrs R. Kodilinye
Chairman, N. R. C. N. D.
c/o Mr. S. M. Ubani
Ag. Chairman, N. R. C. N.D.,
Office of the Bursar,
University of Nigeria

Mrs R. Kodilinye
Chairman, N. R. C. N. D.
c/o Mrs R. U. Egbuono
Works Department
University of Nigeria

OR

Mrs R. Kodilinye
Chairman, N. R. C. N. D.
c/o Mr. P. Menkiti
Vice-Chancellor's Office
University of Nigeria
Nsukka

Mrs R. Kodilinye
Chairman, N. R. C. N. D.
c/o Mrs C. O. Chikwendu
Medical Centre
University of Nigeria
Nsukka

Please Donate Generously!

Yours in the Service to Humanity

R. KODILINYE (Mrs)

CHAIRMAN

NIGERIAN RED CROSS SOCIETY

EAST CENTRAL STATE BRANCH

WOMEN'S SEWING INSTITUTE

Certificate Of Merit

This is to Certify that:

MRS/MISS

has satisfactorily undergone a two-year full-time training course in Dress Making, Embroidery, Cookery, First Aid

AT THE NIGERIAN RED CROSS WOMEN'S DOMESTIC SCIENCE CENTRE, NSUKKA.

R. Koduniye
CHAIRMAN

MANAGERESS

Dated at Nsukka this_____day of_____197____

The response to our appeal was more than we had expected. We had the support of the University staff and local Nigerian builders, who offered free labour or building material. Labour was also offered by the Italian firm, Micheletti, which was at the time building staff quarters on the University campus. I wasted no time and hastily made my way to the local Council Office to 'beg' for a plot of land in the area on which we could build our first motherless babies home. This was the priority, for babies, some only weeks old, were being brought in for our help. The Council obliged and, with their blessing, gave me permission to build our **Dream Home** for the motherless babies.

Fortunately for us, the plot had already been supplied with water and drainage pipes, part of the infrastructure which we would need. Now we could proceed. To do so, however, I had to increase the office staff, and a large room in the University stadium was required for us to meet and discuss further propositions and to hold public functions. We managed to secure the room and appointed more staff: a secretary, a treasurer, a nursing sister from the University Medical Centre, and a financial secretary, together with existing members of the local Red Cross and their field officer. For the social side of the organization, I drew in Boy Scouts, Girl Guides, Cubs and Brownies, with a view to their becoming, after obtaining the 'Proficiency Certificate' (First Aid Certificate), life members of the International Red Cross.

Other members I recruited would be able to obtain the standard Adult First Aid Certificate. We could call upon medical lecturers from the University Teaching Hospital, in addition to nurses and lay instructors, to help with the teaching. We also decided to organize a monthly demonstration on our plot of land, featuring simulated car and cycle accidents, snake bites, emergency calls requiring ambulances, heart attacks and various other emergency situations that the Red Cross might be called upon to deal with. Attendance at these demonstrations was free for members of the public as well as for the trainees. This provided an overall awareness of the work of the Red Cross in the Division.

Everything was beginning to take shape. As time went on, it became necessary to build up our finances. The local young girls who joined us were given free lessons in home economics by the staff of the CEC. The goods they made were put on 'SALE', which we organized on a fortnightly basis and which were held in the stadium. To compensate these young girls, many of whom did not speak English, we paid them according to the amount of satisfactorily made goods they produced. They saved their earnings and, with our help, bought second hand sewing machines which they took home and with which they were able to continue the production of goods in their villages as a means of livelihood, and at the same time to continue to make clothing on a voluntary basis for the Red Cross Sales, from material we supplied to them free. Female University staff members also helped in the teaching of these 'SEAMSTRESSES', as they called themselves, thus ensuring a steady flow of garments, embroidery, sheet sets (the most popular and lucrative), and various other items. Where did the material come from?

I and other appointed officers of the committee made regular visits entailing long journeys up and down the country with the University transport, the use of which we had been previously given. We visited factories as officers of the Red Cross. Since our mission was of a voluntary nature, the factories were liberal with their gifts, and we left each one of them with rolls of material or ends of rolls. All were acceptable for our Red Cross use. We were deeply grateful to them for their generosity.

To quote the old adage, 'All work and no play makes Jack a dull boy', so it was with our Division of the Red Cross. With this in mind, we recruited Brownies, Cubs, Girl Guides and Scouts, who were able to play musical instruments and who, like most Nigerians, had a good sense of rhythm. Whilst training to be Red Cross members, they were able to perform at our various functions and at the same time to train to pass the First Aid Certificate (Proficiency Certificate) and become members of the Red Cross Division, and thereafter to obtain the Standard Adult First Aid Certificate which would earn them a Red Cross badge.

Having increased the Division membership, we then had to provide the members with uniforms to be worn at all times during Red Cross activities. This consisted of white short-sleeved shirts, white trousers, black ties and white overalls bearing the Red Cross, and black shoes and socks. As was to be expected, this would prove to be somewhat costly, so we decided to train the young 'seamstresses' to make these garments. At the sewing classes, which were held three times a week, the girls were taught how to make shirts, ties and overalls from our stock of material donated by the factories. The end result was remarkable. When the uniforms were completed, the Red Cross members blossomed forth at our formal public activities. The divisional Red Cross was now a stamp on the landscape of our Division and we all felt very proud, and indeed our members increased, as did the donations.

In the meantime, the contractors, Micheletti, commenced the building of the motherless babies home on our plot of land. To mark this important occasion, The Hon Justice Agbakoba, Chairman of the Nigerian Red Cross, laid the foundation stone of the building, and the junior members planted the Tree of Progress on the site.

In 1975 Herbert was invited by the Federal Government to build a 300 bed Institute of Ophthalmology to serve West Africa. It was therefore necessary for me to tender my resignation to

Justice Agbakoba and sadly I did so. However I was able to leave my office in the hands of my well trained officers and the work continued.

By 1975, Herbert had reached retirement age and was looking forward to a more relaxed life with his family. This, however, was not to be, for Colonel Obasanjo, Chief of Staff, Supreme Headquarters, in Lagos invited him to establish an Ophthalmic Hospital of 300 beds to serve the needs of Nigeria. Letters bearing on this matter follow in the next chapter.

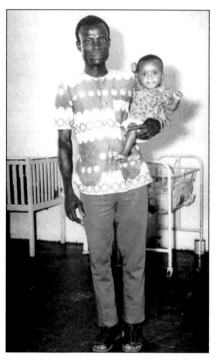

Rosaline Ojoba and Father Jonathan in the baby's home.
Rosaline the subject of our appeal

Chairman Nsukka Division Red Cross saying goodbye to baby Rosaline
as she leaves the motherless babies home in Enugu 1972

Baby Show. Babies from Nsukka Town selectioning the prizes

Twins at the Red Cross Baby Show

U.N.N. Baby Show
Distributing powdered milk to the needy by Red Cross members

Red Cross Members at a demonstration on a plot of land given for the building of The Motherless Babies Home

*Justice Akbakoba laying the foundation stone for the Red Cross
Motherless Babies Home Nsukka Division on our plot of land*

*Laying foundation stone at the Motherless Babies Home at
Nsukka Division*

Chapter 19

National Eye Centre

Publications by **Herbert C Kodilinye**

(1) *'Retinoblastoma in Nigeria: Problems of Treatment'*, American Journal of Ophthalmology, March 1967.

(2) *'Cases of Familial Macular Dystrophy'*

(3) *'Hereditary Congenital Cataract'*

(4) *'Marfan's Syndrome'*

(5) *'Unilateral Buphthalmos and Papilloedema in Hypertension'*, Transactions of the Ophthalmological Society.

(6) *'Understanding Glaucoma'* Dokita-University College Hospital, Ibadan, Nigeria, April 1966.

(7) *'Lymphoma (Lymphoblastoma) of the Lacrimal Gland Treated with Chemotherapy (Endoxan)'*, West African Medical Journal, April 1966.

THE NATIONAL EYE CENTRE INSTITUTE OF OPHTHALMOLOGY

On the 25th September, 1975, Herbert received a communication from the Chief of Staff Supreme Headquarters "to establish an ophthalmic hospital with a view to giving clinical service and training at all levels in the ophthalmological field".

This was a formidable and most responsible assignment, even for one who had spent practically the whole of his professional life in ophthalmology, having been a consultant ophthalmic surgeon for over 24 years, in the United Kingdom and in Nigeria where he had occupied the Chair of Ophthalmology continuously for over twelve years.

The letter read:

Dear Sir,

Establishment of Ophthalmic Hospital

I am directed by the Head of the Federal Military Government and Commander-in-Chief of the Nigerian Armed Forces to invite you to establish an ophthalmic hospital with a view to giving clinical service and training, at all levels, in the ophthalmological field.

You are requested to produce a comprehensive and detailed working paper to include location, staff equipment, different stages of development and cost as soon as possible.

During the planning stage, you will have an office at the Cabinet Office, Lagos, and you should report directly to the Chief of Staff, Supreme Headquarters.

Yours faithfully.

The reply given by Professor H.C. Kodilinye was:

Dear Sir,

<u>Establishment of Ophthalmic Hospital</u>

I am most grateful to the Head of the Federal Military Government and Commander-in-Chief of the Nigerian Armed Forces for inviting me to establish an ophthalmic hospital with a view to giving clinical services and training at all levels in the ophthalmic field. I gladly accept the invitation.

Let me assure His Excellency that I shall do all I can to establish an institute of which our country will be proud. All I need is his full support and blessing in the undertaking.

I must also express my deep appreciation to the Federal Military Government for the confidence it has reposed in me to execute this project in the interest of the nation.

Yours faithfully,

Prof. H.C. Kodilinye.

Letter to Chief F.R.A.Williams

Chairman, Provisional Council

University of Nigeria.

24th September 1975

My dear Chairman,

As it has pleased the Federal Military Government to request me to undertake a new special assignment, I write to tender my resignation as Vice-Chancellor of the University of Nigeria.

Since the University has been completely rehabilitated and reconstructed following its destruction as the result of a disastrous civil war, and since it has been transformed into one of the leading universities in the country under my leadership, I feel I can with confidence hand over to whoever may be appointed in my place.

I take this opportunity to thank the Federal Military Government and the Governments of the East Central State and the South

Eastern State for giving me the opportunity to serve the country in my capacity as Vice-Chancellor of our great Institution.

May I also express my sincere appreciation to the Provisional Council for the support I have at all times received from it. I could not have achieved much without such support.

It will be my constant prayer that the University will grow from strength to strength and continue to play a major role in national development.

Yours sincerely,

H.C. Kodilinye.

Reply by Chairman of Provisional Council:

My dear Vice-Chancellor,

Thank you for your letter of the 24ᵗʰ September, 1975.

I shall bring the contents to the attention of the Provisional Council and will write you further as soon as possible.

In the meantime, I would like, on behalf of this institution, to express the appreciation of the University Community in general and the Provisional Council in particular, for your very valuable services as Vice-Chancellor since the end of the civil war. I wish you success in your new assignment.

Yours very sincerely,

F.R.A.Williams,

Chairman, Provisional Council.

Having accepted the invitation to build an Institute of Ophthalmology in Nigeria, Herbert was allocated a group of university staff to help in the initial stages. Priority was to select the area in which to site the National Eye Centre. Accompanied by some of his staff, Herbert travelled widely throughout Nigeria for some weeks and finally decided that Kaduna, in the North, was the most suitable. It was of great importance that the Institute of Ophthalmology should be sited to meet the following criteria:

(i)   The area had to be accessible to all parts of the Federation of Nigeria, taking transportation into account;

(ii) The area of land allocated had to be large enough for the building of the Institute. About 1,500 acres of land would be required for the full development of the hospital, including lecture rooms, laboratories, student and staff quarters, and for future development; the area had to be accessible for easy movement of patients, students, staff and equipment; climatic conditions had to be suitable;

(iii) The area had to be one where blindness and eye diseases were most prevalent.

KADUNA

Kaduna is the capital of Kaduna State in North Central Nigeria. The city, situated on the Kaduna River, is a commercial and industrial centre and a major transportation hub for the surrounding area. It has a population of 302,000. It is a rail and road junction and the trade centre for the surrounding agricultural area. A pipeline connects the city's oil refinery and petrochemical plants to oil fields in the Niger River Delta.

The city was founded by the British in 1913 and became the capital of Nigeria's former Northern Region from 1917 to 1967. It remains one of Nigeria's most important political centres. Training colleges for teachers, police and the military, two universities and a technical institute are located in Kaduna.

The Kaduna River, the main tributary of the Niger, rises in the Jos plateau and flows for 550 kilometres through Nigeria. It acquired its name from the crocodiles that lived in the river and surrounding area. 'Kaduna' means crocodile in the Hausa language. There are rail and road bridges at Zungeru and at Kaduna, the largest town on the river.

Two areas of Kaduna State were identified on entomological grounds to be Onchocerciasis infested.

ONCHOCERCIASIS (RIVER BLINDNESS)

Onchocerciasis is an insect-borne disease caused by a parasite, *onchocerca volvulus*, and transmitted by black flies. It is often called 'river blindness' because the black fly which transmits the disease abounds in fertile riverside areas that frequently remain uninhabited for fear of infection. Onchocerciasis volvulus is almost exclusively a disease of man. Adult worms live in nodules in a human body where the female worms produce high numbers of first-stage larvae known as *microfilariae*. They migrate from the nodules to the sub-epidermal layer of the skin, where they can be ingested by black flies. They further develop in the body of the insect from which more people can be infected. Eye lesions in humans are caused by *microfilariae*. They can be found in all internal tissues of the eye-except in the lense-where they cause eye inflammation, bleeding and other complications that ultimately lead to blindness.

Onchocerciasis is a major cause of blindness in many African countries. 99% occur on the African continent, with about 300,000 people permanently affected. The disease has in the past greatly reduced economic productivity in the infected areas and left vast tracts of arable land abandoned. It is estimated that there are about half a million blind people due to river blindness in West, East and Central Africa, and world-wide about 18 million people have Onchocerciasis. It spreads through the bite of the female black flies that breed in water. Programmes to control the spread are in place. Onchocerciasis is a non-fatal disease that has caused blindness: a life-long human suffering.

THE NATIONAL EYE CENTRE DECREE 1979

The information that Kaduna was the selected area for the Institute of Ophthalmology was relayed to Supreme Headquarters and was accepted. The National Eye Centre Decree was subsequently promulgated, in 1979. The Decree established the National Eye Centre, comprising a post graduate medical school and a teaching hospital specializing in ophthalmology for the prevention and cure of eye defects and diseases and the prevention of blindness. The Decree also established a Council which would be the governing body of the Centre, and an Academic Board which would have responsibility for the Centre's academic affairs.

Designation

The organization was to be known as Nigerian Institute of Ophthalmology-a post graduate medical institute.

Purposes

(1) To organize and carry out the postgraduate training of medical practitioners as ophthalmologists, and to assist in the teaching of medical students.

(2) To act as a centre for research in ophthalmology.

(3) To train ophthalmic nurses.

(4) To advise the various Governments of the Federation on matters relating to ophthalmic diseases and the prevention of blindness.

(5) To conduct refresher courses in ophthalmology for medical practitioners.

(6) To provide clinical facilities and serve as consultative to other hospitals in the Federation.

(7) To disseminate knowledge of ophthalmology by propaganda through the press, radio and television.

Administration

(1) The Institute shall be administered by a Board of Management and there shall be a Dean who shall direct the academic, research and clinical activities of the Institute.

(2) Composition of the Board of Management:

    (i) Chairman appointed by the Federal Government;

    (ii) Five persons appointed by the Federal Government as board members, one from each of the following Regional Governments-Federal, Northern, Eastern, Western and Mid-Western, and the Dean of the Institute and, at a later stage, members of the Institute to be appointed.

After the signing of the Decree, the Board of Management was appointed, with Alhaji El Kanemi as Chairman, M.D. Yusuf, Chief Inspector of Police (Federal), and one representative from each Region in the Federation. Thereafter meetings were to be held in Kaduna where the National Institute of Ophthalmology was to be built.

A block of buildings was acquired to include the Board Room. These were refurbished and made ready for use. I gathered together a group of young ladies to take on the cleaning of the offices on a permanent basis. Finally the electricity was turned on. Fait accompli-work began.

I was thanked by the Board of Management for my 'service' by the following letters:-

MRS R. KODILINYE

LAGOS

31st August 1982

REF: NEC/CON/120/VOL.11/311

Dear Mrs Kodilinye

Letter of Thanks

I am directed to inform you that the Chairman and members of the Management Board of the National Eye Centre decided at the meeting held on the 15th July 1981, that their most sincere thanks be conveyed to you for sewing and fixing up the window and door blinds in the Centre's office blocks and Board Room at 11 Sambo Road, Kaduna, as well as for organizing the cleaners to tidy up the Board Room in readiness for meetings held on the

14th and 15th of July 1981. Members were delighted for being able to make use of their own Board Room for the first time.

Furthermore, the Board decided that the cost of your flights to and from Kaduna in connection with the meetings held on the 14th and 15th of July should be refunded to you.

Yours faithfully,

(Secretary to the Board of Management, National Eye Centre)

and

Mrs R. Kodilinye

40 Akin-Adeshola Street

Victoria Island

Lagos

REF:NEC/CON/120/VOL.11/312

Dear Mrs Kodilinye

Letter of Appreciation

I am directed to inform you that your various contributions, including the secretarial duties which you undertake, towards the progress of the National Eye Centre have been noted by the Management Board of the National Eye Centre.

In this connection, the Board unanimously decided at its meeting held on the 2nd June 1982 that this letter be addressed to you to express appreciation for your relentless efforts and voluntary services.

The Board was also grateful for the prompt action you took to ensure that NEPA restored the supply of electricity to the Board Room on the 10th August 1982.

Yours faithfully

(Secretary to the Board of Management, National Eye Centre)

With the colonization of Nigeria and the setting up of clinics and hospitals in various parts of the country, modern medicine gradually overtook the traditional medicine, although the latter was still practised quite successfully alongside the modern in some rural areas. Further funds were provided by the Federal Government of Nigeria and there are now at least thirteen Government Hospitals, to mention a few: University College Hospital (UCH) in Ibadan (Herbert created the Chair of Ophthalmology there in 1962), the Enugu Teaching Hospital (also created by Herbert) which became the University of Nigeria Teaching Hospital in 1971, and the Institute of Ophthalmology in Kaduna, to provide for the treatment of eye diseases and blindness (also created by Herbert).

to the best of my knowledge, whilst I am writing these memoirs, looking back over more than 30 years, the situation may have changed.

Since ophthalmology was not a popular specialist course for Nigerian doctors at that time, Herbert realized that it was imperative that Nigeria should send overseas, on government scholarships, young qualified doctors to train as ophthalmic surgeons, a three year course, and to return to Nigeria with a view to replacing the ophthalmic surgeons and nurses recruited from Europe on a temporary basis.

The Federal Military Government was in agreement. Young medical doctors were selected and sent abroad on scholarships. The Government meanwhile appointed NECCO, the Nigerian Engineering Company, to be responsible for the creation of the Institute and ENERGOPROJECT, a Yugoslav Consortium, as the builders under the able hands of 'CHEDA' the Project Manager. The building was soon well in hand. The progress of the building of the Institute would be better understood in pictures, so it is my intention to give a pictorial history of its development from the empty plot of land in Kaduna to the completion of the Centre in 1985, together with the laying of the foundation stone by the Honourable Mr. D.C. Ugwu, Minister of Health on the 31st October, 1980.

For me the laying of the foundation stone was a great occasion, as it was the final edifice Herbert created in his country, Nigeria.

WHO CAN NOW SAY THAT HE WAS 'AN ENGLISHMAN WHO DID NOT WISH TO RETURN TO HIS COUNTRY'?

The National Eye Centre, Kaduna
The Director of the National Eye Centre
Professor H. C. Kodilinye
Requests the pleasure of company of

at the
Foundation Laying Ceremony
of the
National Eye Centre,
Mando Road, Kaduna.
by
Honourable Mr. D. C. Ugwu
Minister of Health
on 31st October 1980, at 10.00 a m
Guests to be seated
at 9. 30 a m.

R. S. V. P.
Regrets only

The National Eye Centre Kadona, Nigeria 1985

The National Eye Centre Kadona, Nigeria 1985 – Completed

The National Eye Centre Waiting Room, Kaduna, Nigeria 1985

The National Eye Centre, Kaduna, Nigeria 1985 – Completed
Foundation Stone laid by The Honourable Mr D.C. Ugwu
Minister of Health

Chapter 20

Biographies

THE HON DR. NNAMDI AZIKIWE P.C. 1904-1996

Dr AZIKIWE (Zik) was born in Zurguru in Northern Nigeria. The son of Igbo parents, he was given the name NNAMDI, which means 'my father is alive'. Zik spent most of his early days in Lagos, the capital of Nigeria attending the Methodist Boys' High School before leaving for America for further studies. There he attended Havard University, Washington DC and thereafter graduated to Lincoln University, Pensylvania in 1930. In 1933 he obtained his masters degree from the University of Pensylvania after which he worked as an Instructor at Lincoln. He returned to Africa in 1943 and became the editor for the newspaper African Morning Post, a daily paper in Accra, Ghana. This was the beginning of his campaign to free Nigeria from Colonialism. In 1937 he returned to Nigeria and continued to campaign for Nigerian Nationalism by founding the West-African Pilot. His publications expanded and eventually he founded the Zik Group of newspapers which he published in the cities across Nigeria.

From journalism Zik entered politics co-founding with Herbert Macaulay the N.C.N.C. - the National Council of Nigeria and the Cameroons in 1944. In 1951 he became Premier of Nigeria's Eastern

Region. On November 16th 1960 he was made the Governor General and on the same day he became the first Nigerian named to the Queen's Privy Council. With the proclamation of the Republic of Nigeria in 1963 he was appointed the first President of Nigeria.

His time in politics spanned most of his later life, being referred to by his admirers as ' The Great Zik of Africa'.

Many streets, buildings, Institutions of Education, University Campuses and hostels are named after him. The University of Nigeria was his creation. His statue was erected in the centre of Enugu, his portrait adorns Nigeria's five hundred Naira currency note and the airport of the new capital Abuja is called the Nnamdi Azikiwe International Airport.

After the death of his wife Flora, Zik retired to his country home Nsukka, where he continued the publication of his books until he passed away in 1996.

MAY YOUR SOULD REST IN PEASE

1.   GENERAL YAKUBU DAN-JUMMA GOWON Oct 19, 1934-

In December 1978, Major General Yakubu Gowon, Head of State and Commander-in-Chief of the Armed Forces received the honorary degree of LLD from the University of Nigeria. This was a welcome honour which he richly deserved. Since he was compelled by the circumstances of the time in 1966 to assume the duties of Head of State

2.   General Gowon was the Head of the Federal military Government and Commander-in-Chief of the Armed Forces from 1966-1975. His parents were CMS missionaries in the early part of Yakubu's life in Zaria where he grew up and was educated.

3.   He joined the ranks of the Nigerian army in 1954 and a year later he received a commission as a Second Lieutenant. By 1966 he advanced to Battalion Commander rank. During these years he had no involvement in politics and remained strictly a career soldier.

4. After the overthrow of the civilian government by a military coup in 1966 General Gowan became Nigeria's youngest Head of State at the age of 32. It appeared that he was made Head of State by virtue of his background. He was a Northerner, he was neither of Hausa nor Fulani ancestry and he was not of the Islamic faith. As the nation at that time was seething with ethnic tension the young officers decided to elect Lieutenant Colonel Gowan to be the Nigerian Head of State and Commander-in-Chief of the Armed Forces. In 1966 Civil War broke out and the eastern Region seceded from the Federation and declared itself Biafra with Lieutenant Colonel Ojukwu as Head of State and General of the People's Army.

5. As many Nigerian authors have written extensively on the Civil War of 1966-1970 it is not my intention to write on the subject. Suffice it to say that at the end of hostilities General Gowon convened a meeting on mutual ground in Hotel Piccadilly in London. Those present were General Yakubu Gowon representing Nigeria and Dr Nnamdi Azikiwe representing Biafra. Professor H.C. Kodilinye and his son were also present. They declared the secession ended and the country was once again ONE NIGERIA.

6. In December 1978, General Gowon received the honorary degree of LLD from the University of Nigeria. In his Convocation Address, the Vice-Chancellor, Prof HC Kodilinye, had this to say:

7. "Since he was compelled by the circumstances of the time in 1966 to assume the duties of the Head of State and Commander-in-Chief of the Armed Forces, General Gowon, as a man of action, has always demonstrated his selfless dedication to duty. His actions have been guided by his Christian concern for thoroughness with grace. His magnanimity was demonstrated by the humane manner in which he fought the war to keep Nigeria ONE. When the Civil War ended in 1970, General Gowon planned a programme of rehabilitation, reconstruction and development, not only in the war-affected areas but throughout the country.

This included the nine-point programme which was launched in October 1970.

8. With his characteristic dedication to peace, General Gowon has paid personal visits to most of the African countries that supported him during the Civil War to keep his country united, in order to express his gratitude. Trade agreements with other Wesr African countries have been signed. In May 1972 General Gowon was elected Chairman of the Organization of African Unity. With this position he now combines national leadership with leadership of the African continent. During visits to the United Kingdom he appealed to the British Government to ensure majority rule in Southern Africa, and he later went to the UN General Assembly to present the case of the OAU for the recognition of Guinea-Bissau.

---

9. GENERAL CHUWUEMEKA ODUMEGU OJUKWU Nov 4 1933

10. Colonel Odumegwu Ojukwu was born in Zungera, Northern Nigeria. He was the leader of the secessionist state Biafra, which declared itself independent from Nigeria in 1971. Previously he was the military governor of the Eastern Region of Nigeria. Sir Louis Odumegwu Ojukwu KB, his father was a business tycoon and was thought to have been Nigeria's first multi-millionaire.

11. Chukwuemeka's name means 'God has done well'. He was educated at Epsom College in England and later gained his Master's degree in History at Oxford University and finally graduated from the royal Military Academy of Sandhurst.

12. After the collapse of the Civil War Ojukwu, as he was referred to by his people left Biafra and settled in the Ivory Coast (Côte D'Ivoire) where he helped to set up a government in exile, living there for 13 years.

13. President Alhaji Shehu Shagari pardoned Ojukwu and allowed him to return to Nigeria in 1980. Thereafter he joined Shagari's National Party (N.P.N.) and contested the 1983 election for the Senate. In 2003 he ran for the Presidential Election. The writer, Kurt Vonnegut refers to Ojukwu as 'The Nigerian George Washington'.

14. General Odumegwu Ojukwu is now in retirement in Eastern Nigeria.

15. In 2002, General Ojukwu said: "Nothing has happened to change things."

---

16. ALHAJI ADO BAYERO, EMIR OF KANO MUHARRAM 1349 (15.6.1930)

Alhaji Dr Ado Bayero was born on 15 June 1930 in Gidan Rumfu, the son of Sarkim Kano Alhaji Abdullah Bayero. He has become leader of Muslims not only in Kano but also in many parts of Nigeria. He is one of the most respected Nigerians and is regarded as a wise counsellor because of his experience and diverse cultural links that make him a bridge and an asset in promoting mutual understanding and resolving conflicts.

Alhaji Ado Bayero started his working career at the Bank of British West Africa (which later became First Bank) in 1947, and in 1949 he left the Bank to join the services of Kano Native Authority. During his service at the NA, he attended courses in Nigeria at Clerical Training Centre, Zaria, and Local Government Courses in the United Kingdom. He was the Chief Clerk of the Kano Town Council. He joined partisan politics and contested and won elections for the Northern Region House of Assembly under the banner of the Northern Peoples Congress (NPC) in 1954. He made his inaugural speech in the House on 3rd March 1955. He resigned as a member of the House in 1957 and was appointed as Wakilin Doha Chief of Kano Native Authority Police, and after five years in 1962 he was appointed Ambassador for Nigeria to Senegal. He was summoned to Nigeria to become the 13th Emir of Kano, while studying French in Switzerland, in October 1963.

17. He has served in Nigeria in various capacities mainly as the Chancellor of the Universities of Nigeria, Ibadan and Maiduguri. In Kano he has been the force behind the construction of many mosques and Islamic schools. Ado Bayero is the longest serving Emir and his reign has been characterized by prosperity.

GENERAL OLUSEGUN OBASANJO

General Obasanjo was President of the Federal Republic of Nigeria from 1999-200? After retirement, General Obasanjo became the co-chairman of the Commonwealth Eminent Persons Group in South Africa.

CHIEF F.R.A. WILLIAMS

Chief Frederick Rotimi Williams of Nigeria was born to a lineage of lawyers. He was a man of unparalleled devotion to the law and he held the unity of the Nigerian nation very dearly to his heart.

In 1970, he became Chairman of the Provisional Council of the University of Nigeria.

Sadly, he passed away on 20th April 2005. May his Soul Rest in Perfect Peace.

JUSTICE TASLIM OLUWOLE ELIAS

Judge Taslim Oluwole Elias, the former Chief Justice of Nigeria, and the only Chief Justice elected from the Bar, was also the first indigenous Attorney-General of Independent Nigeria.

Judge Elias was at a later stage appointed a Judge at the International Court of Justice in The Hague.

The commemoration of the 10th Anniversary of his death was recently held at his Victoria Island, Lagos, residence. May Your Soul Rest in Perfect Peace.

MR. UKPABI ASIKA

Ukpabi Anthony Asika was a Nigerian academic who later became the civilian administrator of Enugu, and later the East Central State of Nigeria, during and after the Nigerian Civil War. He was the Administrator of the liberated states of Biafra during the Civil War. After the war, he was faced with the challenges emanating from the increase in crude oil revenues and from the reconstruction of the war-ravaged East.

While serving as Administrator, he was the only civilian member of the Gowon Supreme Military Council.

Ukpabi was one of the prominent Igbo sons who joined the Federal side during the war, preferring a unified and modern Nigerian state to a fractured one, and seeking a rational solution to the country's problems. During that time he was sometimes in opposition to friends, relatives and even brothers. To some, his stance on the war made him a symbol of unity and hope for a unified country that could emerge after the war. His cosmopolitan upbringing and academic disposition equipped him with the ability to offer solutions to problems, and his willingness to deviate from the paths followed by the majority may have made him more of an independent force in the East.

Asika was born in Jos, Plateau State, on June 2, 1936. His parents worked in Edo State and his elder brother, Evaristus Asika, a trained lawyer, died in 1949 while returning to Nigeria in a mail boat. Asika was educated at St Patrick's College, Calabar, and Edo College, Benin, before proceeding to the University of Ibadan where he completed his studies in 1961. Prior to going to Ibadan, he worked as a clerk in the Department of Marketing and later with the Northern Nigeria Marketing Board. Asika later attended the University of California, Los Angeles where he earned a masters degree in political science in 1963 and served as the President of the African Students' Association (1963-1965). He joined the staff of the University of Ibadan just a month before the January 15, 1966 coup that led to the emergence of Johnson Aguiyi Ironsi, an Igbo officer, as the Nigerian Head of State. A few months later, a counter-coup brought another army officer, Yakubu Gowon, from the old Northern Region, to power. This coup also resulted in the assassination of Ironsi. Between July 1966 and November 1966 many Igbos were killed, and some in the North and in the West returned to the East, fearing for their lives. Ukpabi decided to stay at the University of Ibadan. Prior to the end of the war, his major duty as Administrator of captured territories was to provide a case for a united Nigeria abroad. After the war he had the responsibility for rebuilding much of the war ravaged East.

BRIGADIER UDUOKAHA ESUENE

Brigadier Uduokaha Jacob Esuene (1936-1996) was a Nigerian air force officer who was Military Governor of South-Eastern State (later renamed Cross River State) between May 1967 and July 1975 during the military regime of General Yakubu Gowon. He was the first governor after the State was formed in May 1967 when Eastern Region was split into East-Central State, Rivers State and South-Eastern State.

Brigadier Esuene was of Ibibio ethnicity and was a fighter pilot before being appointed governor of South-Eastern State. In the run up to the 1993 presidential election, he was a candidate for the presidential ticket of the Social Democratic Party (SDP).

THE HON MR JUSTICE AKBAKOBA

THE HON MR JUSTICE AKBAKOBA WAS THE FIRST CHAIRMAN OF THE FEDERATION OF NIGERIA RED CROSS SOCIETY (N.R.C.S) WHICH WAS FORMED IN 1960 AND HAS ITS HEADQUARTERS IN LAGOS.

It has over 600,000 volunteers and 300 permanent employees. The Nigerian Red Cross Society was established by an Act of Parliament in 1960 and became the 86th member of the National Society of the League of Red Cross and Red Crescent (now International Federation of Red Cross and Red Crescent Societies) on 4 Feb 1961.

MR. DONALD CAMPBELL. CBE

DONALD CAMPBELL WAS BORN IN HORLEY, SURREY, ON 23RD MARCH 1921. HE WAS THE SON OF SIR MALCOLM CAMPBELL, HOLDER OF 13 WORLD SPEED RECORDS IN THE 1920S AND 1930S IN THE FAMOUS BLUEBIRD CARS AND BOATS.

He attended Uppingham School.

Like his father, Donald Campbell was a renowned British car and motor boat racer. Many of his record-breaking attempts took place on Coniston Water in the English Lake District. Donald in fact broke 8 world speed records in the 1950's and 60's. He remains the only person to set both land and water speed records in the same year (1964).

He was killed on 4th Jan 1967 while attempting to break his own world record.

DR. HASTINGS KAMUSU BANDA 1906-NOVEMBER 1997

Dr Hastings Kamusu Banda completed his medical education in Great Britain and became a very successful General Practitioner in Liverpool during the 1930's-1940. He later returned to his home country (then British Nyasaland). Like many African leaders, he spoke against colonialism and helped to lead the movement towards independence. In 1963 he was appointed Nyasaland's Prime Minister and led the country to independence as Malawi a year later. Two years later Malawi was declared a republic with Hastings Banda as President. Being politically minded he consolidated power and declared Malawi a one party state under the M.C.P (Malawi Congress Party). In 1970 the M.C.P. declared him the Party's President for life and in 1971 he became President for Life of Malawi itself.

As an educationalist he decided that Malawi should have a famous Public School like Britain. The building was completed and later it was named the 'Eton of Africa. Banda made it known that anyone wishing to enter this co-educational school must be prepared to read Latin and

Greek. If they were not prepared to do so they would not gain entry. The school was staffed with teachers drawn from well known British Public Independent schools and discipline was seriously enforced. At the time of writing this school still exists.

As a leader of the pro-Western block in Africa Hastings Banda received support from the West during the Cold War. He supported women's' rights, improved the country's infrastructure and maintained a good educational system. During his time in office he was a state guest of the Queen. He died in South Africa in 1997, although this date is controversial.

THE RT HON SIR MILTON MARGAI DEC 1895-APRIL 1964

Sir Milton Margai was a Sierra Leonean politician and the first Prime Minister of Sierra Leone. He was the main architect of post colonial Sierra Leone and guided his nation to Independence in1961. He was born in the Southern Province of Sierra Leone. His country at that time was a British Protectorate. His father was an affluent businessman. Sir Milton was educated at the Evangelical United Brethren School in Bonthe, the town in which he was born and his secondary education took place at the Albert Academy in the capital Freetown.

In 1921 he was the first Sierra-Leonean to graduate in Fourah Bay College as Bachelor of History. Thereafter he went to England where he qualified at King's College in 1926 at the University of Durham. He was the first Protectorate man to become a medical doctor.

After qualifying in Medicine in Newcastle he married and lived in Monks Eaton, a seaside resort just outside Newcastle and it was here that Sir Milton, Herbert, Joy and I used to play tennis doubles in the late 1930's. Sir Milton and his wife had two daughters.

Sierra-Leoneans regard Sir Milton Margai as a man of honesty and high principle. His time in office was a period of prosperity and social harmony. Sir Milton is looked upon as the only post-Independence leader of Sierra-Leone, admired and respected by Sierra-Leoneans.

In 1961 he built a school for the blind in Freetown, the motto being 'We cannot see but we will conquer'. In 2006 the BBC put on a documentary on the school for the blind and the School for the Blind Choir toured the United Kingdom in 2003 and 2006.

The Right Honourable Dr Nnamdi Azikwe G.C.F.r. Former President
of Nigeria. Responsible for Nigerian Independence from Great Britain
October 1961

Chukwuemeka Odumegwu
Ojukwu, President of Biafra
In office
May 30, 1967 – January 8, 1970

Donald Campbell
23 March 1921

The Right Honourable Sir Milton
Margai M.D. 1st Prime Minister
of Sierra Leone
In office
April 27, 1961 – April 28, 1964

Hastings Kamuzu Banda
1st President of Malawi
In office
6 July 1966 – 24 May 1994

*Alhaji Ado Bayero, C.F.R.,
Hon. LL.D. (Nigeria) His
Highness, the Emir of Kano
Chancellor, University of
Nigeria*

*His Excellency, Dr Ukpabi Asika,
B.Sc. (Lond.), M.A. (U.C.L.)
Hon. LL.D. (A.B.U.), Hon. (D. Lit)
(Nigeria) The Administrator of
the east-Central State of Nigeria
Visitor, University of Nigeria*

*Chief F.R.A. Williams, M.A.
(Cantab.,) Q.C. of Gray's Inn
Barrister-at-Law, Chairman
of the Provisional Council,
University of Nigeria*

*His Excellency, General Yakubu
Gowon, Hon. LL.D., (Nigeria)
Head of State and Commander-in-
Chief of the Armed Forces Federal
Repubic of Nigeria, Visitor to the
University*

His Excellency, Brigadier U. J. Esuene Hon. LL.D. (Nigeria) The Military Governor of the South-Eastern State of Nigeria Visitor, University of Nigeria

Chapter 21

The Grandchildren

RUSSELL'S REMEMBRANCES OF GRANDAD

In everlasting memory of my dear Grandpa who slept in the Lord on 21st September 2003. I write these few words to say how grateful I am for the wonderful opportunities you gave me in my life.

At the age of 7 years, you registered me to attend St. George's School, Windsor Castle; then, at the age of 11 years I attended Haileybury School in Windsor; and finally, at the age of 14 years, you arranged for my admission to Harrow School, Harrow-on-the-Hill. When I reached the age of 18, on completion of my secondary education, I entered the University of Manchester and later worked in the history museum there.

I take this opportunity to say "Thank you" from the bottom of my heart. I will endeavour at all times to uphold the good name of the Kodilinye family.

May your "Soul Rest in Peace"

From Russell, your loving Grandson.

HENRIETTA'S CHILDHOOD RECOLLECTIONS OF GRANDPA

Tea at the Overseas League was always a great event. We would travel into London on the Metropolitan line train, bouncing our way along to Baker Street. Grandpa would wear a smart suit and his cosy Russian hat and Grandma would be very elegantly dressed and we would all troop to the Overseas League in fashionable St. James's. Tea would be an elegant affair with a selection of sandwiches and other good things. Grandpa would always insist on having his sandwiches without butter but Grandma and I would be far more interested in the cream and jam scones.

The garden at Hatch End, where they lived was huge and perfect for playing in. A large evergreen and a cherry tree made a convenient football goalpost and after a lot of persuasion, Grandpa even joined in once to take some penalties. He loved to play "tag" with me, chasing in and around the apple trees, but I remember cheating by hiding in the "secret passageway" behind a long, thick rhododendron bush.

At Christmas time, my parents and I would go to Hatch End and eat a huge turkey feast, cooked by Grandma and beautifully laid out in the dining room. Afterwards, we would retire to the drawing room to open our presents. Grandpa would sit there with a happy smile on his face admiring pretty wrapping, reluctant to disturb it, while the rest of us ripped ours open enthusiastically.

My grandfather's musical tastes were eclectic, to say the least. He was very fond of listening to the group Abba as well as Eddie Grant and used to make tape of them for me. He loved his musical collection and would spend hours sorting and re-sorting out his tapes in Nice.

When Grandma was lying in a French hospital in Nice with a broken knee after falling down a hill, Grandpa trawled me around the markets for ages looking for some strawberries to take to her as they were her favourites and he wanted to cheer her up.

MARIA'S RECOLLECTIONS OF GRANDPA

Grandpa had a glittering career and was one of the most accomplished people I have ever known. My respect for him is immense and enduring and I know that I am not alone in this regard.

From his Vice-Chancellorship at the University of Nigeria, Nsukka, to his postgraduate studies at Oxford University, he placed a premium on excellence and hard work that even the most diligent would be hard-pressed to emulate. I have always thought that if I could achieve even half of what he did in his lifetime, I could safely consider myself a success.

Grandpa was not just a surgeon, but was also a teacher. He had formal teaching experience at tertiary level, but he also informally taught those who looked up to him by the example he set.

Two things Grandpa taught me are the value of education and the importance of taking pride in oneself, and those are lessons I will carry with me for the rest of my life. He was firm and disciplined but his sternness belied a kind heart and a concern for improving the position of others to whose life he could make a difference. This concern acted as a compass by which he was guided throughout his life and career.

For all his achievements, my fondest memories of Grandpa are rather humble. They range from the mundane (the odd eye test he would administer) to the quirky (his pink dressing gown and partiality to impeccable dress, even at home). My most vivid image of Grandpa is of him sitting at the head of the dinner table, talking to the family about his time in Nigeria and the people he knew and worked with there. Anyone who knew him can attest that he was not just a great man and accomplished doctor, but also a great Grandpa. He was, and continues to be, respected and loved dearly.

MATTHEW'S MEMORIES OF "GOOD OL' GRANDPA!"

Good ol' Grandpa. I do not remember much of him but since his death in 2003, I have grown to understand and appreciate his life history and all of his accomplishments, especially in Nigeria to which he devoted his time into making it a better place. When I say "Grandpa" what am I reminded of? There is one story that I remember vividly and it goes like this:

One day, I was sitting in front of the television watching a VCR tape in the living room. It was Lion King. This is the movie that I would sit down and watch over and over again and would never grow tired of it. Behind me was, as I remember, a rather frail man sitting on the couch with a thick red covered book in his hands and a magnifying glass that was sharply in focus of the black and white print. He raised his head from the face of the book and fixed his eyes onto me.

"Where are your parents?" he said in his clear Nigerian accent.

"They are sleeping," I replied.

"*Neeping*, what is *neeping*?" he said.

"No, they are sleeping."

His voice raised as he became irritated and he said, "*Neeping*, there is no such word as *neeping*!" and he lowered his head to continue reading his book. Desperate to prove my sanity, I made one final attempt to make him understand and I said,

"They are upstairs *sssssleeping*."

His fading eyes returned to my face and he shouted

"Silly boy, there is no such thing as *neeping*!"

Just then, I heard the door swing open. Not knowing who it was, I ran towards the door only to find good ol' granny back with her groceries. I was happy that she had returned so that she could save me from Grandpa's powerful words. I explained the situation to Grandma and when she processed it, she let out a great laugh that was reminiscent of the Queen of England's! A rather amused grandmother carefully rested her groceries down by the door and walked over to the living room to confront my accuser.

"Grandpa, Gilbert and Vanessa are having a rest," she said.

"Oh, they are resting. Okay then," he replied casually and he returned to his literature. I was rather dumbfounded that Grandma had solved the problem so simply and with that, I returned to the television hoping that I had not missed my favourite parts of the movie.

Looking back, I know that I was sitting in front of a man who had been through so much in his life. I know that Grandpa was an honourable and respectable man who had built the first eye hospital in Nigeria and had survived civil wars and uproars which included cataclysmic air strikes and plummeting passenger planes. Although his ears were losing their sensory perception and his eyes were fading rapidly to the point where he had to use a huge hand lens, his thirst for knowledge was never quenched. He would read and read and read for what seemed like a never ending rollercoaster. I was not alive to see him in his healthier days and to witness the hard work he put in to help others, but I know his determination, devotion and diplomacy would have made him an excellent professor, doctor, friend and father. He came across to me as a perfectionist which is, indeed, a very useful trait in the field of medicine where precision is a necessity. Although I don't know very much about Grandpa Herbert, Iknow that he is a credit to our family, his community and his nation. His hard work, great accomplishments and powerful presence will, unlike his disintegrated body, never fade away. Good ol' Grandpa.

JESSICA AND GRANDPA

Since I was too young to remember Grandpa (I was only two years old when he passed away), I can only say what my brother, Matthew, has told me about him. Matthew told me that Grandpa used to enjoy holding me on his lap and would say how pretty I was. He would carry me into the garden and stand under the apple tree while he watched the older children kicking a football. He thought I looked a bit like his mother when she was young. I know that Grandpa loved all his grandchildren, and I wish I could have known him when he was alive.

Epilogue

A RARE VISIT TO THE EYE CENTRE

It was some time in Autumn 2006
Since I visited the Centre upon promise to Lady Ray Kodilinye, widow
of Prince Kodilinye
The Founder of Kaduna Eye Centre

I hold my breath
Trying not to cry

As I look around in the darkness of the night,
The moon and stars
Parading high above the sky,
With recollection going through your thoughts

Wishing that I knew you long before.

Let a centre be built: those were his very own words

The emphasis and focus were largely to build an Eye Centre, where it
would serve those that matter

Nigerian Odyssey

A sight is born and
A centre is born
A sight is real
A sight is in the centre
For all North South Eastand West
A sight is where all should visit
A sight is for the future
A sight is for all to heal
A sight is here to stay

Long after Kodilinye is gone
Yet it shall remain for all time

Forgotten we have not
For the selfless service you gave to the Fatherland

The day you left this mortal world to meet with your Lord

Even when I visit your grave
The day I can never forget
In life as in death
Your Lady still stands beside you
Recalling in her very own words:
What a true Nigerian you were and
What service you have given to the fatherland and
How little was mentioned of you
Even in her mid-90's
A challenge she must take by putting words to ink

Perhaps future generations may learn

Always my eyes filled with tears,
Even though I tried to disguise

Epilogue

I truly come to term
Death is merely a transition, but
That which we sew is what we shall reap

Memories are real for they shall never vanish

The great man's name ought to be written into immortality

What happened to our collective conscience in giving credit where credit
is due

Or is it too late to correct the misdeeds of the past?

And remember his wise words
Let the Eye Centre be built...where the majority of the people suffer
from river blindness (onchocerciasis)

His was a dream come true
Today you are no longer with us,
But we shall always remember what you stood for

May your dreams come true and your hopes live forever!

What a star and what a perfect gentleman

May you rest in perfect peace.

Abubakar Sadiq Ajiya (a family friend)
London 21/03/2009

As I lay down my pen I would like to say

LIFE IS NOT A BED OF ROSES
TAKE HEART AND MEET EACH MOMENT
WITH FAITH AND GOD'S GREAT LOVE
AWARE THAT EVERY DAY OF LIFE
IS CONTROLLED BY GOD ABOVE

Experto credite